WINNERS ALL

ANNE HOLLAND has written numerous non-fiction books related to horses and horse-racing, including *The Grand National.*, *In the Blood*, and *Kinane: A Remarkable Racing Family*, all published by The O'Brien Press. She was also a successful amateur rider.

Acknowledgements

With sincere gratitude for all who have helped me with information about the heroes and heroines within these pages: Sean Bell, John Berry, Robert Brabazon, Louise Cooper-Joyce, Kim Dyas, Robert Hall, Horse Racing Ireland, Jessica Harrington, Irish Horse Welfare Trust, Michael Hourigan, Dessie Hughes, Avalyn Hunter, Jeremy James (The Long Riders Guild Academic Foundation), Patrick Joyce, Vali Lancu, Gail List, Michael McCann, Jennifer Moore, Martin Murphy, Aidan O'Brien, Clare Oglesby, Edward O'Grady, Cyril O'Hara, Steve Parrott, Anne Peters, *Racing Post*, Patsy Smiles, Tommy Crompton Smith, Charlie Swan, *Timeform*, Trish Walker, Lee Ann Day-Whistler and Margaret Worrall.

Contents

First published 2012
by The O'Brien Press Ltd
12 Terenure Road East, Rathgar, Dublin 6, Ireland
Tel: +353 1 4923333; Fax: +353 1 4922777; Email: books@obrien.ie
Website: www.obrien.ie

ISBN: 978-1-84717-312-6

British Library Cataloguing-in-publication Data
A catalogue record for this title is available from the British Library

1 2 3 4 5 6 7 8 9 10
12 13 14 15

Layout and design by the Little Red Pen, Dublin
Printed and bound by Scandbook AB, Sweden
The paper used in this book is produced using pulp from managed forests.

Picture credits: *Jacket* [front] Barry Geraghty and Moscow Flyer clear a fence during the Queen Mother Champion Chase Race, 2003 – Julian Herbert/Getty Images; [back] see Plates [4] and [12]. *Plate section* [1] Topham Picturepoint/Press Association Images; [2] Edward Gooch/Getty Images; [3] Hulton Archive/Getty Images; [4] Photo from the Hulton Archive/Getty Images; [5] Popperfoto/Getty Images; [6] PA Archive/Press Association Images; [7] S&G and Barratts/EMPICS Sport; [8] AP/Press Association Images; AP/Press Association Images; [9] S&G and Barratts/EMPICS Sport; [10] Dennis Oulds. Central Press/Getty Images; [11] Chris Smith from the Hulton Archive/Getty Images; [12] racingpost.com/photos; [13] Martin Lynch, Doncaster. Mirrorpix; [14] PA Archive/Press Association Images; [15] Anne Grossick, racingpost.com/photos; [16] Patrick McCann, racingpost.com/photos; [17] PA Archive/Press Association Images; [18] Mirrorpix; [19] racingpost.com/photos; [20] PA Archive/Press Association Images; [21] Patrick McCann, racingpost.com/photos; [22] racingpost.com/photos, Mirrorpix; [23] racingpost.com/photos; [24] Edward Whitaker, racingpost.com/photos, Mirrorpix; [25] Tony Marshall, EMPICS Sport; [26] AAP/Press Association Images; [27] Tony Feder, AP/Press Association Images; [28] Jae C. Hong, AP/Press Association Images; [29] Jae C. Hong, AP/Press Association Images.

WINNERS ALL

Favourite Racehorses
Through the Years

Anne Holland

THE O'BRIEN PRESS
DUBLIN

Introduction

W rite us a book about the twelve best racehorses through time,' the publisher asked. Not possible, I countered. For one thing, such a list is opinion-based rather than definitive – and impossible to prove. For another, many of the best horses have already been written about extensively.

We compromised on favourite horses, managed to reduce the 'must-have' to seventeen or eighteen – and then down again to fifteen – but even then there are glaring omissions, as I shall explain.

Going right back to the beginning, I chose the Byerley Turk ahead of his two co-founders of the Thoroughbred breed (the Darley Arabian and the Godolphin Arabian, sometimes called a Barb), not because he was better – that accolade probably belongs to the Darley colt as it is believed that 85 per cent of all Thoroughbreds today trace to him through the male line – but because he had such a heroic story. He was the only one of the three known to have raced, and also the first of the three to arrive on English shores, in the late 1680s, followed by the Darley Arabian in 1704. Some reports give it that he had just a few mares, others that they were numerous; whichever is true, his breeding influence remains great to this day.

The third founding sire of the Thoroughbred was the Godolphin Arabian, imported in 1729 into England by owner Mr Edward Coke and then sold to Lord Godolphin (an early bigwig in the sport of racing). The Godolphin Arabian was to stand at stud at Coke's Longford Hall in Derbyshire, which means that all three founding sires of the Thoroughbred stood in the north of England.

Choosing Eclipse for the eighteenth century was almost a one-horse race – after all, nearly half of his eighteen wins were walkovers! He retired mainly due to lack of opposition, but when it came to stud, he truly proved himself, being still the most influential sire. For the nineteenth century, there may have been better horses than Bend Or, including one or two also ridden by Fred Archer, but the feat of horsemanship in that 1880 Derby will possibly never be bettered. St Simon, Ormonde (sired by Bend Or), Persimmon and others only receive passing mention 'in dispatches', much as they deserve a chapter to themselves.

As for the Grand National, Manifesto was easy to choose as my nineteenth-century winner, as the only horse in the great race's history worthy of comparison with Red Rum, but in the twentieth century I hate to omit the likes of Troytown, Cloister, Reynoldstown, Red Rum himself and Australia's magnificent Crisp.

That brings us to more recent times and the most glaring omission from this book. Arkle is, after all, most people's favourite racehorse as well as the best horse over fences of all time. I apologise, but, as the fiftieth anniversary of his first Cheltenham Gold Cup approaches, watch this space. And how could I leave out the same stable's Prince Regent and Flyingbolt? The answer is possibly because I have included a number of horses from modern times, within more readers' memories, than those from past decades. Certainly it is well known that it was some time before Tom Dreaper conceded that Arkle was better than Prince Regent, who, in spite of a career interrupted by the Second World War, won the 1942 Irish Grand National and the 1946 Cheltenham Gold Cup.

Flyingbolt was hugely talented but was unlucky to contract brucellosis, a nasty and fairly unusual illness for a horse. A tall, wishy-washy (pale) chestnut with a broad white blaze, he was unbeaten over hurdles in his first season and also in his first season steeplechasing. At the Cheltenham Festival of Arkle's third Gold Cup (1966) he not only won the (now Queen Mother) Champion Chase but the next day turned out again and failed narrowly to win the Champion Hurdle as well. Later the same season he won the Irish Grand National giving lumps of weight away. He was a chaser of the highest calibre who combined Champion Hurdle speed with Grand National stamina, and it was a shame indeed that, as a stablemate of Arkle, they were never to meet in the Gold Cup (unlike Denman and Kauto Star in recent times).

Golden Miller, with five Cheltenham Gold Cup wins in the 1930s (when the Grand National was still the premier race), and Best Mate, with three, have also failed to make my final cut. Likewise Long Run, in whom we had thought we quite possibly had the most plausible candidate to be mentioned in the same breath as Arkle. The sight of Long Run swinging down the hill and round the corner on the heels of the previously dominant pair, Kauto Star and Denman, in the 2011 Cheltenham Gold Cup, and sweeping past them in mid-air at the final fence, drawing clear on the uphill finishing straight, was truly one of those magical moments.

Dawn Run did my own burgeoning career no harm a quarter of a century before that, but is another to be left out this time. I wrote an updated chapter on her in *In the Blood* (2009). Dawn Run's win in the 1986 Gold Cup is the stuff of legends, and even today, watching the replay, it is 'impossible' for her to get up to win from her third place over the last fence, especially having cut out the running to that point. Yet, galvanised by Jonjo O'Neill, she did. Her career ended in tragedy, but she should be remembered for winning the Champion Hurdles of England, Ireland and France in 1984, and that momentous Gold Cup of 1986, as well as the famous Match at Punchestown where, in Tony Mullins' hands, she beat Mouse Morris on lifelong rival Buck House.

Another public favourite was Desert Orchid – Dessie – but his story, too, is well told elsewhere. It is left to the great post-war Cottage Rake to represent the Cheltenham Gold Cup, and, apart from establishing trainer Vincent O'Brien's arrival on the world stage, Cottage Rake's story is itself fascinating, not least that he failed the vet three times. That did not dissuade the sage O'Brien.

Another brilliant but tragic horse, for different reasons to Dawn Run, to be left out is Shergar. Those who saw his incredible ten-length Derby victory of 1981, ridden by the then teenager Walter Swinburn, knew they had witnessed greatness. The broad white blaze on his bay head drew further and further ahead of his talented rivals. He added the Irish Derby and the 'King George' to his record but failed in the St Leger and was retired to the Aga Khan's Ballymany Stud, Co. Kildare, only to be kidnapped and believed murdered with just one crop of foals on the ground.

Also on the flat, Sea The Stars is another I have omitted on this occasion. It is hard to imagine a more complete racehorse, and it was wonderful to write a book on him in 2009. Sometimes flat horses that sweep all before them in the spring and summer of their three-year-old season become hyped up as 'horse of the century' then fail in the autumn. Not so with Sea The Stars. Not only did he win the 2,000 Guineas in May and the Derby in June, along with three other Group 1s that summer, but he went on to win October's Prix de l'Arc de Triomphe in what was one of the most outstanding racing feats of all time, extricating himself from a seemingly hopeless boxed-in position. Many previously unblemished reputations have been lost in the 'Arc', but Sea The Stars proved himself quite possibly the best racehorse of all time. Both his sire, Cape Cross, at four, and his dam, Urban Sea, at five, improved with age, and what Sea The Stars could have further achieved in future years can only be conjectured. It was an inevitability of the commercial flat game that he would be retired to stud. When HM Queen Elizabeth II paid her historic visit to Ireland in May 2011, she included two private stud visits, and one of them was to visit Sea The Stars at HH The Aga Khan's Gilltown Stud, and some of his first foals.

In more recent times, Vinnie Roe, winner of four Irish St Legers, and Yeats, four times victorious in the Ascot Gold Cup, were two extremely popular horses with the public. A statue to

Yeats was unveiled by the Queen on the opening day of Royal Ascot 2011.

I had two difficult pancakes to toss on the National Hunt scene: Danoli or Dorans Pride and Florida Pearl or Beef Or Salmon: a quartet of Irish favourites spanning most of the 1990s and much of the first decade of the new millennium. Between them they lightened many a winter's afternoon of National Hunt racing. It has come down on the side of Dorans Pride and Beef Or Salmon.

Danoli, trained by Tom Foley in Bagnalstown, Co. Carlow, was named after his owner, Dan O'Neill and his daughter Olivia, and was a brilliant hurdler who made a good transition to chasing but with some jumping lapses. In fact, he was never out of the first four in all his completed races, but he also notched up four falls and one unseated rider in his career total of thirty-two races. Probably his greatest win was the 1994 Sun Alliance Novices Hurdle at the Cheltenham Festival, followed by back-to-back Martell Hurdles at Aintree, and the highlight of his chasing career was winning the 1997 Hennessy Gold Cup at Leopardstown where he beat Jodami. In retirement, Danoli was on view to an adoring public as companion to Michael Smurfit's Melbourne Cup winner, Vintage Crop, at the Irish National Stud, until Danoli suffered a fatal attack of colic in April 2006.

It was equally hard to leave out Florida Pearl, a beloved part of National Hunt racing from 1996 to 2004. A great favourite with the public and trained by the incomparable Willie Mullins, the bay with a distinctive broad white blaze is remembered not only for his three-timer in Leopardstown's prestigious Hennessy Gold

Cup between 1999 and 2001 but also, even more remarkably, for staging a momentous comeback by retaking the trophy three years later in 2004.

For Australia, the triple Melbourne Cup winner Makybe Diva's incredible story is here, and at the other end of the distance scale I have included sprinter Black Caviar with an undefeated twenty-two wins at the time of writing, at the end of Zenyatta's story. They are three incredible mares.

As for Frankel, trained by Sir Henry Cecil in Newmarket, we have the complete racehorse. He took his unbeaten score to six when running away with 2011's 2,000 Guineas, making all and scoring by a dominant ten lengths. He had set off in front in the manner of a pacemaker, but he simply did not come back to the vainly pursuing pack. At Royal Ascot that June he made it seven from seven, though on this occasion the winning post may have come only just in time for him, but he impressed for win number eight in the Sussex Stakes at Goodwood. At Ascot's new Champions Day on 15 October 2011, Frankel franked his superiority in the £1 million Queen Elizabeth II Stakes. The good news for racing was that he would stay in training as a four-year-old, a sporting gesture by his owner Prince Khalid Abdullah who could simply have retired his colt to stud.

A minor injury scare in spring 2012 put racing again in jeopardy but since then, at the time of writing, Frankel has added the Lockinge Stakes at Newbury and, in as great a flat-racing display as most racegoers have ever seen, the Queen Anne Stakes at Royal Ascot in June. At four he has matured, settled – and improved. Irish-born jockey Tom Queally only had to let out an inch of rein to forge an eleven-length gap between himself and his nearest pursuers at Ascot. The Qipco Sussex Stakes at Goodwood in August brought a glorious twelfth, beating the supplemented Fahr in facile fashion at odds of 1–20 in front of a crowd of 25,000, and becoming the first colt ever to win this race in successive years. At the time of this book going to press he is due to go up in distance from a mile to 10 furlongs for the first time in the Juddmonte Stakes in York; he appears certain to take it in his great stride. It is hard to imagine seeing as perfect a racehorse again – and to think he is only two years younger than Sea The Stars. As the doyen of racing commentary, the ninety-four-year-old Sir Peter O'Sullevan, quipped afterwards, 'That was worth staying alive for.'

There is also Camelot, winner of the 2012 2,000 Guineas and Epsom Derby, who, by the time this book is published, may have taken the elusive Triple Crown. At the end of June 2012 he added the Irish Derby to his Classic portfolio on ground so heavy that only four rivals took him on, of which Sea The Stars' three-parts brother, Born to Sea, tried to make a race of it. Camelot has proved a credit to his late sire, Montjeu, as has his jockey, Joseph O'Brien, to his father, Aidan, who with this win took his haul of training Irish Classic winners to twenty-eight, surpassing Vincent O'Brien's long-held record. So the sport of racing has, as ever, much to look forward to, both on the flat and over jumps.

It is my hope that readers enjoy my chosen equine stars through racing history.

The Byerley Turk

A savage storm rages in the hills surrounding the remote Balkan village; the thunder claps reverberate around the forest-clad circle of hills like a furious god, and the rain falls straight in torrents, drenching any person or animal caught out in it in seconds.

Most of the village inhabitants are curled up asleep, oblivious to the battle in the sky. A child cries, momentarily frightened, and is soothed by its mother, and they sleep again; their milch cow and assorted hens are warm and dry in the open-sided basement beneath them. Outside, in the rough stable, a mare is thrashing on the ground, soaked in rain and sweat. Soothing and encouraging her is a groom, oblivious to the downpour, as he helps her bring her foal into the unfriendly world.

A flash of lightning illuminates a dark head emerging from the labouring mare. The colt is black, with not one bit of white on him. It is 1679, and the colt is destined to be known as the Byerley Turk, one of the most influential horses throughout the history of competitive horse racing.

It is quite possible, perhaps even probable, that the colt was in fact born on one of the massive Turkish studs in the Karaman area of Turkey where feudal 'squires' or *timars* worked on a military meritocracy, breeding horses as chargers for the wars that were a seemingly endless feature of this part of the Balkans as the Ottomans struggled to cling to power.

Huge state studs called *hirashi* reared many different strains of quality Turkish horses, the most widely used being the Karaman, at 16 hands plus. There were also specialised centres – *yund* and *tayçi* – devoted to the rearing of young stock.

The *timariot* system could produce 200,000 mounted men on command, riding highly schooled, big, beautifully bred horses without the Sultan putting a hand in his pocket. The horses were not produced for money: they were bred as a state requirement. This was what honourable men did. Naturally, rivalry between *timars* was intense and therefore ensured an ongoing improvement in the quality of horseflesh.

A traveller to the then mighty Ottoman Empire, Robert Bargrave, wrote that he had 'never seen such horses, and that in great number, as all Christendom cannot vie with; many of whose accoutrements alone are worth thousands, and those are common which cost less than hundreds. [. . .] The most inferior of them would in England be the greatest gallants.'[1]

The people of the Ottoman Empire were descended from the horsemen archers, including the Cumans, Uigars, Kazakhs, Uzbeks, Huns, Turkmenians, Petchenegs, Khazars, Khabars, Oghuz and Selçuks. It was in their blood to breed many large, quality horses. It is said that the Turkish clans of western Siberia, notably the Kipchaks, owned in excess of 2 million horses, and of the Uigar Turkik clan, there was a contemporary saying that 'the number of horses only God knows.'

The steppe land provided perfect conditions for quality horse breeding: abundant land, grass and water of the river plains of the Amu Darya, the Syr Darya, the Volga, the Ural and the Ember. The steppe itself, made up of the Ferghana, the foothills of the Pamir, the Khorosan and the High Mazandaran, was constantly rained upon. The horse breeders pushed west. They came with Tamerlane and with Genghis Khan, with the Selçuks and plenty of others besides. It was the Turkish Huns who sacked Rome. Foreigners were forbidden to buy the Turks' horses, and the only way they ever left the Ottoman Empire was either by stealing, smuggling or as a spoil of war.

Wherever he was actually foaled, the story that the Byerley Turk was born in a thunderstorm, leaving him fearless amid the noise and tumult of battle, has survived the centuries. The magnificent nearly-black colt saw army service within a few years of his birth. The Ottoman Turks were forced out of Vienna in 1683,

---

1 R. Bargrave, *The Travel Diary of Robert Bargrave, Levant Merchant (1647–1656)*, London: Hakluyt Society, 1999.

when the horse was four years old. His saddle and bridle would have been studded in diamonds and rubies. His *sipahi*, or cavalry officer, would have been equally glittering from top to toe in his Ottoman uniform, probably in the open-fronted tunic of red, with white belt and red girdle and black leather boots, and plentiful jewels as well.

History mentions the colt in the hands of a Turkish cavalry officer and an archer groom. The archer and the colt were ideally matched, for both possessed fiery minds, unafraid of anything or anyone. The horse was so fleet of foot and seemingly unafraid – certainly not of cannon-fire – and the archer so accurate with his aim that between them they appeared invincible.

The battle in September 1683 turned against the Ottomans when the Polish cavalry mounted the biggest charge ever seen, of some 20,000 horses. It was led by the King of Poland, Jan III Sobieski, heading the 3,000 heavy lancers known as Winged Hussars, after the appendages on their armour.

It must have been a daunting sight, even to the Byerley Turk.

Before the charge, the King called upon the protection of the Blessed Virgin Mary, and later Pope Innocent XI named 12 September, the date of the battle, as the Feast of the Holy Name of Mary. The West inherited a number of other cultural legacies from the siege of Vienna. Among the items abandoned by the defeated Ottomans were a number of musical instruments from their military bands. The triangle, cymbals and bass drum had not been seen before in the West but have been used in orchestras ever since. Also, it is believed that croissants, shaped in the crescent emblem of the Turkish flag, originated from the time of the siege.

In France, certain types of bread and buns are known as Viennoiserie to this day. As for the cappuccino coffee popular today, it was after the victors found bags of coffee stored in the abandoned Ottoman camp that they added milk and honey to it to make it taste less bitter . . .

With the Turks ousted from Vienna, the Holy Roman Emperor, Leopold I, gathered around him, with the Pope's blessing, a Holy League and set about pushing the Turks out of Hungary, too.

Although the Byerley Turk survived Vienna (assuming that is not where he was captured, as some sources have suggested), his life was to change in another battle also fought on the banks of the Danube. In 1686, the black horse and his archer groom found themselves in the thick of battle above the city of Buda, which was divided from its sister town, Pest, by the river. History does not relate what happened to either the archer or the cavalry officer, but we do know that the black horse, on the losing side, was captured as a prize.

Fighting for Leopold's Holy League was one James Fitzjames, and it was he who, unbeknownst to him, won perhaps the best war trophy of all: the black Turkish horse, which was to become known as the Byerley Turk – the first of the three acknowledged foundation progenitors of the Thoroughbred horse line.

It is possible that on the boat for England the colt's companion may have been a grey Turk, the Lister, en route to the Duke of Berwick. What a sight they would have made: black and white together. It is also possible that the two horses met again, for both were present at the battle of the Boyne.

When Fitzjames returned home with his trophy, either he was looking for a quick buck or he underestimated the value of his prize, or his acquisition was simply seconded into the army, for the next we know is that the horse was partnered with Captain Robert Byerley of the 6th Dragoon Guards, formerly the Queen Dowager's Cuirassiers, a crack mounted regiment that only admitted horses which were bay and generally considered superior. (The Byerley Turk's official colour would have been bay or brown – there are very few true blacks.)

The Turkish horse was not only bigger than the two Arabians that were to follow him into Thoroughbred history a few years later, but he would also have been taller and finer than most English horses of the time. Unlike the Godolphin (14.1½ hands high), and Darley (15 hands) Arabians, he was at least 16 hands and, even allowing for artistic licence, had a long back, plenty of bone and masses of heart room (as did both Eclipse and Arkle in later years). His neck was elegant, and he had a beautiful head with long ears, big eyes and a commanding presence.

Robert's father, Col. Anthony Byerley of Middridge Grange, Co. Durham, had been a cavalry officer under Charles I, whose unit was known as 'Byerley's Bulldogs'. It is easy to imagine that Robert had a good eye for a horse and a hunger for a fight. An officer still in his twenties, Byerley was lucky enough to find the Turk much more than a mechanic of war: he was a sentient animal in whom he could find and replicate that most important understanding between man and horse: confidence – the trust, quick wit and ability that between them each could get the other out of trouble. By the time Byerley was twenty-eight he had risen to the rank of lieutenant-colonel and he knew how good the Turkish horse beneath him was. He may have spent most of 1689 in Ulster and possibly took part in the siege of Carrickfergus Castle. A year later, in March, he was in Downpatrick, Co. Down, where he and two other officers decided to race their horses. It might have been just another race between officers but for two things: one of the participants would be remembered for posterity and King William himself would give his name – and money – to the race, which became a regular fixture.

Byerley intended to win that day. His horse was already well known in Hounslow Barracks and Whitehall Palace stables and was considered something of a mascot in England.

Ulster already boasted a number of good horses, for breeding had been encouraged five years earlier by King James II when he founded the Down Royal Corporation of Horse Breeders to improve horse breeding in the county. The Down Royal races were run on an undulating 3-mile horseshoe-shaped track at Downpatrick, not dissimilar to the course near there today.

It is believed that Col. Byerley's Turk and his opponents, possibly Col. Heyford's Barb (Royal Dragoons) and Col. Hamilton's borrowed cob (20th Lancashire Fusiliers), started their race from the crossroads outside the Flying Horse pub, Downpatrick. Soldiers from all three regiments gathered to support their respective leaders – and to lay wagers. A man called William Hill opened up a book; today, the string of betting shops bearing his name are synonymous with book-making. There were strict rules for the race, which forbade contestants to whip or unhorse or to use swords against each other. Spectators were not allowed to throw missiles at them, and the race was to be run on a clean circuit that the contestants had walked in advance. It was probably in the region of 3 miles. One source puts Col. Heyford's Barb as the winner, and while that may be more reliable there is a story of the race that has come down the centuries as told by the Governor of Hillsborough Castle to King William and unearthed by Jeremy James, author of *The Byerley Turk*. As the story goes, the Byerley Turk arrived at the start awash with sweat, reared high into the air when the starting pistol shot and promptly galloped off in the wrong direction, to the dismay of his 6th Dragoon supporters. By the time he got back on the right course, his rivals were half a league – about 1½ miles – ahead. He set off in what appeared to be vain pursuit.

> With the end of the race looming it still appeared that no magic on earth could secure Colonel Byerley the King's Plate, and yet on he galloped, gaining lost ground by the stride. On and on the horses thundered and then witnesses beheld a most remarkable thing.
>
> It was as if Byerley's Turk took wing. [. . .]
>
> Suddenly the great Turk horse went hurtling past Colonel Hamilton's Cob and with the end of the race in sight, he was narrowing the gap on Colonel Heyford's Barb with every stride.
>
> Not a hundred paces lay between them and the end of the course and soon they were galloping neck and neck. Then another kind of energy seemed to fill the limbs of the Turk: as if some magical power overcame him; as if some wondrous elixir coursed in

his veins. He shot past the Barb and took the finishing line with a length to spare. The 6th Dragoons went insane with joy.[2]

After hearing this story, King William declared that the race should take place annually, called it the King's Plate and endowed it with £100 in perpetuity. It is still an annual event. Recent winners of the contest, usually run over 1 mile 5 furlongs, include horses trained by John Oxx (four), by Sir Mark Prescott from Newmarket (two), by Dermot Weld (two), as well as by Aidan O'Brien, David Wachman, Jim Bolger, Noel Meade, M. J. Grassick and, most recently, V. C. Ward. In 2011, 'Her Majesty's Plate' was won by Northgate, trained by J. G. Murphy and ridden by P. J. Smullen. In 2012, the race was won by Chicago for trainer/jockey combination Aidan and Joseph O'Brien.

It is early in the morning of 1 July 1690, just below Oldbridge, Co. Meath. The mist begins to rise off the river Boyne, wide here, not long before the end of its journey that began on the bog in Co. Offaly; a couple of miles further on it spills into the Irish Sea at Baltray, west of Drogheda. As the mist rises, two huge encampments are revealed on either side of the dark width of water. William's army is spread out beneath Tullyallen on the west bank, and James's is on the east near Oldbridge.

Col. Byerley is despatched to reconnoitre the enemy James's positions. He rides through William's ranks first, noting their

---

2   Jeremy James, *The Byerley Turk: The True Story of the First Thoroughbred*, Ludlow: Merlin Unwin, p. 286.

preparedness for battle. Their new-fangled flintlock muskets are polished and ready, the men are well fed and in good spirits, all 36,000 of them. There are food wagons and replacement weapons at the rear, along with a fully functional hospital. Other medical posts are placed at strategic points throughout the camp.

Byerley bows as he passes the King's wooden war headquarters. Designed by Christopher Wren, it is complete with war room, dining room (all the best silver) and bedchamber. William's standard is flying, denoting his presence. When Marshal Schomberg, struggling with losses from both disease and battles such as Carrickfergus, requested reinforcements, the King himself had come over to Ireland to take command. He brought with him 300 boats of troops (the elite of Europe), 2,500 draft horses, an artillery train and 550 wagonloads of supplies.

William's goal was Dublin, and the forthcoming battle on the banks of the Boyne was a mere stepping stone to that end.

As he rides on, Col. Byerley notices that the enemy has destroyed the bridge near Slane, but he and the Turk ford the river higher up – it is deeper than he expected – and boldly ride on, heading towards Oldbridge and James's camp. What he sees is a ragged army numbering some 23,500 in total. Not only is it noticeably smaller but he takes in at a glance how untrained and ill equipped most of the men are. Their matchlock muskets will, he knows, be inadequate. It is likely that many will not work and those that do will be fatally slow compared with William's flint-locks. They would fire only three shots per minute, and in the agonising seconds between each reloading the infantrymen would have only pikemen to defend them. To Robert's surprise, and no doubt inner delight, he saw that many of the men – they looked like farm labourers – were armed only with scythes and pitchforks, hardly a match for the Williamites.

Robert had ventured too close. Suddenly he realised he was almost surrounded. He wheeled the Turk around, dug him hard in the ribs with his spurred heels and galloped flat out to escape – a slower horse and he would have been captured.

King William himself also had a close shave the day before. Both sides were encamped and ready for battle, but it was a Monday, a day on which, traditionally, it was considered unlucky to fight. When King William, mounted on his milk-white horse, was out on a reconnaissance with the Prince of Denmark and the Duke of Ormond, he was grazed by a cannon ball. It is said that he commented, with masterly understatement, 'It was as well it came no closer.' Had he been killed the course of Irish history might well have been different.

Next day, 1 July 1690, the battle of the Boyne began. The date was in the old Julian calendar and is equivalent to 11 July in the Gregorian, although the commemoration of the battle is held on 12 July. The Jacobites, for all their shortcomings, gave it their best shot. There were periods in that day when fortunes swung to and fro like a pendulum, and victory hung in the balance either way.

Upstream, 17,000 Jacobite dragoons fought the Williamites – possibly the Byerley Turk among them – ferociously. The Jacobites' number two, Sir Neal O'Neill, was killed, demoralising those around him. William's number two, Marshal Schomberg, had been dealt a similar fate early in the battle. The dragoons on both sides advanced towards each other, only to find themselves held back by a ravine, looking on helplessly, the Jacobites with pieces of white paper in their hats, the Williamites with a sprig of green in theirs.

Meanwhile, downstream, where the tidal river was at its lowest point, King William's Dutch Blue Guards crossed the water eight to ten abreast, holding their muskets over their heads. In places the water rose to their armpits. William was with them. His beautiful horse got stuck in the mud and had to be pulled clear by the men around him.

At this point, the Byerley Turk is more likely to have been upstream with the dragoons, facing increasingly depleted Jacobite opponents. The bulk of the Williamite army advanced on them. It looked as if the Jacobites were about to be surrounded. Staring defeat in the face, King James, far from rallying his troops, beat a hasty retreat – briefly to Dublin and then back to France via Duncannon and Kinsale, leaving victory at the Boyne to King William. James's men fought on for another year, with battles such as Aughrim, until signing the Treaty of Limerick in 1691.

Robert Byerley, meanwhile, returned home to Middridge Grange, Co. Durham, to marry Mary Wharton in 1692. Naturally he brought his princely black charger with him, where he stood at stud for a number of years. After the death of Robert's father-in-law, Lord Wharton (himself a keen horse-breeder), the Byerleys moved, in 1697, to Goldsborough Hall in North Yorkshire, their stallion with them, to deserved luxury.

It is believed that the Byerley Turk did not have all that many 'bred' mares (as opposed to commoners) while at stud, but luckily there were enough to make their mark. Basto, a colt born in 1702 and probably one of the Byerley Turk's last foals, was to prove one of his best. Like his father, Basto was nearly black, and he was not only a good racehorse but also a good sire. Probably the most influential son of the Byerley Turk was Jigg, who in turn sired Partner. It was Partner's son Tartar who sired Herod.

Foaled in 1758, Herod was leading sire eight times. Owned and bred by Prince William Augustus, the Duke of Cumberland, third son of King George II, Herod – or King Herod as he was sometimes known – was reared at the Duke's Cranbourne Lodge, Windsor Great Park. The Duke, incredibly, also bred Eclipse, the pair being two of the best and most influential sires of the Thoroughbred.

Herod was not as dark as his great-grandfather but, like him, he had almost no white, bar a small star. He was a big, well-made horse, who possessed those crucial qualities in a racehorse, speed and gameness. He won most of his races over the (then normal) 4 miles, at Newmarket and Ascot, beginning as a five-year-old.

At stud, Herod established the importance of the Byerley line through many notable descendants, including the 1780 inaugural Epsom Derby winner Diomed (sixteen wins from twenty-three races), who was by Florizel. Herod also sired Highflyer, who was unbeaten in fourteen races, and whose sons were champion stallions twenty-three times in twenty-five years. Herod was himself the leading sire in Great Britain eight times, from 1777 to 1784, at which point his son Highflyer took over. In time, his son, Sir Peter Teazle, also went on to lead the list a number of times, up to 1809.

Today, of the three founding stallions of the Thoroughbred line, it is the Byerley Turk who has come perilously close to extinction – saved, possibly, by the top Irish sire Indian Ridge, who stood at the Irish National Stud. Indian Ridge, who died of a heart attack in 2006 at the age of twenty-one, ranks as the most recent top-class European stallion to have descended in the male line from the Byerley Turk.

Writing on the Thoroughbred Internet in June 2011, John Berry says,

> It would possibly be premature to say that this line is in terminal decline (not least because there are several good sons of Indian Ridge at stud) but, even so, the death of Indian Ridge was as serious a blow to its prospects as had been the death of Rubiton in Australia the previous year. However, as Indian Ridge and his own sire Ahonoora both proved, great sires can come from seemingly unlikely backgrounds, so the next great Byerley Turk-line sire could be lurking just around a corner.
>
> If the full extent of Indian Ridge's success at stud was hard to predict (which it was), then even more unexpected was the extraordinarily successful stud career enjoyed by his sire Ahonoora. By the time that Ahonoora retired to stud in 1980 after a productive career spent contesting Britain's top sprints, the future of the Byerley Turk sire-line in Europe appeared to lie in the hands of stallions who were most notable for siring either middle-distance gallopers or stayers. The excellent stallions Klairon and Levmoss (winner in his racing days of both the Prix de l'Arc de Triomphe and the Ascot Gold Cup and who was shaping as a top-class sire prior to his early death at the age of only twelve) had died in 1975 and 1977 respectively, but

the likes of Blakeney [Epsom Derby], Luthier and Rarity (and in turn several sons of Blakeney) were all stallions who might be looked upon to come up with Classic contenders. By contrast, Ahonoora, who had won the 6 furlongs Stewards Cup at Goodwood as a three-year-old in 1978 and the Group Two William Hill Sprint Championship (which is now the Group One Nunthorpe Stakes) at York at four, was a far less obvious candidate to prolong the line.[3]

Interestingly, Cape Cross is out of an Ahonoora mare and was the sire of possibly the most complete Thoroughbred racehorse of all time, Sea The Stars, as well as the outstanding mares Ouija Board and Seachange. Two sons of Indian Ridge, who are both stallions and can therefore help continue the line, are Compton Place (July Cup in 1998) and Namid.

Down the centuries, descendants of the Byerley Turk have won just about every type of race across the world, from classics such as the Epsom and Kentucky Derbys, to sprints, to races such as the Melbourne Cup on the flat, and the Grand National, the Irish Grand National, the Cheltenham Gold Cup and the Maryland Hunt Cup over fences.

The magnificent Byerley Turk died in 1714, at the age of twenty-five. Clare Oglesby, the present owner of Goldsborough Hall, told me, 'As far as we understand, the Byerley Turk was buried in the grounds of Goldsborough Hall. It is said that it was

---

3   See http://www.thoroughbredinternet.com/newsmore.html?Id=17524 (accessed 31 May 2012).

under a newly planted tree within a stone's throw from the stable block. We have two possible locations for the site, under a very large copper beech tree or under a very old whitebeam which fell down a couple of years ago. We haven't yet got round to a plaque but it is on the "to do" list!'

The legacy of the Byerley Turk lives on. One interesting hypothesis, to racing people in general and Irish breeders in particular, has been propounded by scholar and author of the fictional *The Byerley Turk*, Jeremy James, who writes:

> That blood, that size, the shape, that speed came from the Turk and it is to be remembered with some sobriety that this stallion spent two years in Ireland from 1689 to 1691. And what realms of improbability are there to imagine that a young stallion of this kind of potency hacked from one end of the country to the other as a celibate for two long years? We need to take another long look at the Irish descended bloodlines and consider precisely what they are, and what, precisely, are their real historical roots, based upon factual evidence and not upon enthusiasm for a breed in the absence of dispassionate research.[4]

---

4 Jeremy James, 'On the Foundation Turks', The Long Riders Guild Academic Foundation: The World's First Global Hippological Study, http://www.lrgaf.org/articles/foundation-turks.htm (accessed 31 May 2012).

2

Eclipse

The Byerley Turk was said to have been born in a fierce thunderstorm, and so it was that another of the most influential racing stallions of all time was also said to have been born during a natural event. Eclipse may have been foaled during an eclipse – either in March or April 1764. If not born during the eclipse, he was certainly named because of it.

Many Arabian horses, and Turks, too, were imported to England between 1660 and 1750, but the direct descendants of the three foundation stallions contributed most to the breed as we know it today: Herod (the Byerley Turk), Eclipse (the Darley Arabian) and Matchem (the Godolphin Arabian, sometimes called Barb).

Owned, as was Herod, by the Duke of Cumberland, Eclipse was a bright chestnut with one long white stocking on a hind leg and a white blaze down his head. He was unbeaten on the racecourse but was never champion sire, finishing second no fewer than eleven times, usually to his stable companion and his senior by six years, Herod. His influence on Thoroughbred breeding was equally great, if not more so, and his racing record was impeccable.

While Herod was from the Byerley Turk line, Eclipse was a great-great-grandson of the Darley Arabian (born in 1700) on the sire side, while his dam, Spiletta, was by Regulus, an unbeaten son of the third foundation sire, the Godolphin Arabian.

Small and thickset, the Godolphin Arabian was born in Yemen, exported to Tunis and from there was sent as a gift to King Louis XV of France but apparently not appreciated. The story, probably fictional, is that he then pulled a cart through the Paris streets before one Edward Coke bought him for £3 and brought him to England. Then Coke died, aged only thirty-two, and the horse passed to Francis, 2nd Earl of Godolphin. The horse suffered further indignity by being employed as a 'teaser' at stud, testing to see if a mare was ready before she was taken off to the 'main man'. A mare called Roxanna rejected the intended stallion so the Godolphin Arabian was given his chance, and, far from spurning him, Roxanna produced one of the era's great horses, Lath (nine wins from nine runs). The mating continued, producing another good horse in Cade and finally, best of all, Regulus. All three carried their sire's colour and conformation – much as Sadler's Wells' sons do today.

The Darley Arabian was imported to England in 1704 from Syria, but only after subterfuge. He was reared in the desert outside Aleppo, among the herds and tents of the Fedan Bedouins, where he already had a name – either Manak or Manica – probably from the Muniqi strain of Arabians renowned for their speed. (It seems strange that he did not keep his name.) He was owned by Sheikh Mirza II, and the fine bay colt caught the attention of the British Consul, Thomas Darley, a merchant and member of a local hunting club. One story says that Thomas Darley arranged for the purchase of the yearling colt for 300 golden sovereigns for his brother Richard. Thomas Darley then learned that the Sheikh had reneged on the deal, claiming that he couldn't bear to part with his finest colt. Thomas Darley felt that a deal was a deal. He arranged with some sailors to acquire the colt by their own means and to smuggle him out via Smyrna, and that is apparently how the young stallion arrived in England, in 1704, to take up stud duties at the Darley family estate, Aldeby Hall, near Leeds.

The colt, now known as the Darley Arabian, stood 15 hands high and was the lightest in colour of the three founders, with considerable white on him. Portraits show him as extremely elegant with a long, fine head, white blaze and two white socks on his hind legs and a snip of white on a front one.

Once in Yorkshire, the colt embarked on stud duties mainly for his owner, but a local mare, Betty Leedes (by Old Careless), was allowed to visit him. She produced the full brothers Flying Childers (six wins from six runs, three of them walkovers) and the unraced Bartlett's Childers, champion sire in 1742. Old Careless was a chestnut with two white hind legs and a white blaze.

It is through this Childers line that the Darley Arabian became the great-great-grandsire of Eclipse, by Marske, born in 1750. It might never have been: Marske's sire, Squirt, suffered from the painful foot condition laminitis, and his owner, John Hutton, instructed that he be put down. A groom intervened and saved the horse.

Marske was bred by John Hutton at Marske Hall, Yorkshire (many of the early notable breeders were in the north of England), but he exchanged him as a foal for an Arabian owned by King George III's brother, Prince William, Duke of Cumberland. On the track, Marske won the 1754 Jockey Club Plate in Newmarket and a 300-guineas match, but he did not win again and was retired to stud two years later at a low fee. He stood at the Duke's stud until his owner died in 1765, when he was part of the dispersal sale.

By 1750, the new taller, larger and faster Thoroughbred horse had become an established breed, averaging 16 hands in height and capable of speeds of up to 40 miles per hour and covering 20 feet or more in a single stride.

The rapid expansion of horse racing created a need for a central governing authority, and, in 1750, racing's elite met at Newmarket to form the Jockey Club. They drew up and regulated the complete Rules of Racing and sanctioned racecourses to conduct meetings under those rules. Forty years later, in 1791, the first volume of *The General Studbook* was published, listing 387 mares – all descendants of the three founding stallions.

A year after Eclipse was born, his owner died, and Cranbourne Lodge and all its bloodstock had to be dispersed by auction sale.

This included Herod, Marske and the yearling by Marske listed as Lot 29. Although he was to grow to 15.2 hands, a good height for this era, Eclipse was an ungainly, gangly yearling, similar to many a human teenager, and did not draw a lot of interest. He was a chestnut, not always a popular colour, and had quite a bit of white on him, including a stocking on a hind leg, which was likely to make him even less attractive to some men's eyes. A wealthy Smithfield butcher and cattle dealer, William Wildman, had set his heart on him. Wildman already owned Gimcrack, winner of twenty-six of his thirty-three races, so it may be assumed that he had a good eye for a horse. He had bought the small grey for £35 and tried to resell him for 15 guineas, but once Gimcrack started winning Wildman sold him to Lord Bolingbroke for 800 guineas. Like Eclipse, as we shall see, he too had a famous race named after him (the Gimcrack Stakes, at York's summer meeting, the 'Royal Ascot of the North'), after which the winning owner traditionally delivers the speech at the Gimcrack dinner.

Many stories survive around some of these early horses, not all of them true. One, which may or may not be true, is that William Wildman insisted on the sale being restarted. When he arrived he found the bidding had started ahead of the advertised time and that the colt he wanted had already passed through the ring for 75 guineas. Wildman insisted that the lots sold up to then be reoffered, and, after some negotiation, he was able to bid for the colt. Some accounts say that the bidding reached 70 or 75 guineas and that it took only one more bid before the colt that would be called Eclipse was his. A document of the Royal Veterinary College put his price at 45 guineas. Whoever the colt had originally been knocked down to had, for the briefest of times, owned but then lost the horse of the century.

In the same sale, Herod was bought by Sir John Moore and stayed in training for a couple more years before retiring to stud at the age of eight. Marske made just 26 guineas, and his new owner, Lord Bolingbroke, stood him at his stud in the New Forest for a fee of just 3 guineas. When Marske was eighteen years old, Wildman bought him for 20 guineas and stood him at a fee of 5 guineas. Once Eclipse stormed onto the racing scene, the covering fee rose, first to 10 and then to 30 guineas.

Wildman then sold Marske to the Earl of Abingdon for 1,000 guineas, a 4,900% mark-up, but the Earl recouped this within one covering season, first by raising the stud fee to 50 guineas and then to a top whack of 100 guineas.

After his sale, Eclipse was broken and 'tried'. This meant testing him on the gallops, to see what ability he might have before entering him for a race. The task was not straightforward: Eclipse proved fiery, excitable and intractable – so much so that at one time the option of gelding him was considered. Just imagine: no horses descended from Eclipse! Castration can sometimes be the answer for a horse with his eyes and heart on things other than racing – usually the fillies or sometimes just plain laddishness – which means that his racecourse performances are poor. A case in point was Istabraq: had he not been gelded it is extremely unlikely that he would have won three Champion Hurdles.

Before resorting to gelding, William Wildman sent the spirited colt to nagsman George Elton in Epsom. A nagsman is someone unafraid of a difficult horse, who will knock off the rough edges and 'make' him. The colt was sometimes 'ridden all day and occasionally all night as well'.[1] (Night-time poaching forays with the youngster apparently led to Elton's transportation in due course, possibly to Maryland or Virginia.) Nothing would break the colt's spirit or his determination – it wasn't that he was bad-tempered, rather that he was high-spirited. He ran with his hind legs wide apart (as Arkle was to do), powering him forward, and with a head carriage so low that he sometimes appeared to be almost sweeping the turf with it.

At that time, horses usually began racing at the age of five years, and most races were over 4 miles, including qualifying heats, all held one after the other. It was also quite usual for a horse showing ability at home to be given his pre-race trials in secret, away from the touts. Betting was for many the raison d'être of horse racing, and, then as now, connections would, if they could, keep a good price for themselves. So it was with Eclipse, and his trial, held at dawn, might well have remained unknown had it not been seen by an old woman who was out on the Downs that early. Once the racing touts arrived they badgered her for information. She told them that she had seen a horse with a white leg 'running away at a monstrous rate', the other horse so far behind that she was sure it would never catch up 'even if he ran to the world's end'.[2] There have been 'talking horses' – those with a big reputation at home but who don't then live up to it on the racecourse – throughout the history of horse racing, but the prediction for Eclipse proved correct.

---

1   Nicholas Clee, *Eclipse: The Story of the Rogue, the Madam and the Horse that Changed Racing*, London: Bantam Press.
2   Clee, *Eclipse*, p. 86.

The secret was out, and the punters' money resulted in odds of 1–4 for the chestnut's racecourse debut on his home track of Epsom on 3 May 1769, a Noblemen and Gentlemen's Plate for horses that had not won £30 (matches excepted), to be run in 4-mile heats, for five-year-olds and upwards, £50 to the winner.

Racing, known as the sport of kings, has always been embraced by all-comers and has always attracted colourful characters. One such was an Irishman, Dennis O'Kelly, from Tullow, Co. Carlow. If his story is to be believed, O'Kelly came to England as a young man seeking his fortune, working first as a sedan chairman, carrying the wealthy about London. While doing so he chatted up a bored and wealthy countess; she took him into her service – and her bed. All was well until her husband found out, and O'Kelly was promptly sacked.

The experience had developed in him a taste for the high life. He next gained employment at White's Chocolate House, where he gambled recklessly and, before long, was in the Fleet Prison for debt. This time it was a brothel-keeper, Charlotte Hayes, who came to his rescue, and it was she, apparently, who financed his entry into racing, in addition to his gambling. On the other hand, in his book *Eclipse and O'Kelly* (1907), Theodore Cook maintains that O'Kelly was not the ruffian he has been made out to be but that he had 'learned a good Italian hand', that is, he was probably well enough educated to possess graceful handwriting.

O'Kelly was among those present at Epsom for Eclipse's first race, and he had apparently already made himself known to Wildman, even providing the trial horse for Eclipse. Now he was so impressed with the way Eclipse won his first heat, beating Gower,

Cade, Trial and Plume, that he determined to own him. He did not have sufficient funds, so he bet that he would correctly place all the runners in the next heat. His bet, which has become a part of racing lore, was, 'Eclipse first and the rest nowhere.' To be 'nowhere', a horse had to be 'distanced', that is, to finish at least 220 yards (a furlong) behind the winner.

There was an interval of just half an hour between heats, during which time the horses were rubbed down before setting off once again on their 4-mile race. For the first 3 miles, Eclipse stayed with his opponents, head low, stride long, but he was toying with them. As his jockey John Oakley allowed him to stretch on, the gap between Eclipse and his rivals became longer and longer, and he drew away to win by 'a distance'. Not only did this mean that O'Kelly had won his bet, but it also meant that Eclipse had won the race outright without the requirement to run yet another 4-mile heat.

With his winnings O'Kelly franked his confidence in the horse by acquiring, first, a half-share in him for 650 guineas, and the following year he paid a further 1,000 guineas to buy him outright.

Just under four weeks after his first race, Eclipse contested his second, this time at Ascot. Horses were walked from course to course at this time. The race was another Noblemen and Gentlemen's Plate for £50 to the winner, but, for the only time in Eclipse's career, this one was over 2 miles. Eclipse didn't find it difficult to beat Crème de Bauble (Cream de Barbade).

In June he was at Winchester, back over 4 miles. This, on paper at least, was more competitive. There were six runners in the first heat, after which both Caliban (owned by O'Kelly – an early case of a pacemaker, one wonders?) and Clanvil were 'distanced', eliminating them from the second heat. The order of finish was the same as for the first heat: (1) Eclipse, (2) Slouch, (3) Chigger, (4) Juba. Eclipse's exertions won his owners another 100 guineas. Two days later, at the same venue, no one was willing to take him on, and Eclipse notched up his first walkover and another £50 in prize money.

On consecutive days at Salisbury at the end of June it was more of the same, though this time the walkover was on the first day, for 100 guineas, and Eclipse then saw off Sulphur and Forrester the next day, for 30 guineas and a silver bowl. At the end of July, he walked over for 100 guineas in Canterbury, and two days later, on the South Downs above the little Sussex town of Lewes, he beat his sole opponent, Kingston, in both heats to earn another 100 guineas. Eclipse ended his season by winning 100 guineas at Lichfield, where the heats were over 3 miles, beating Tardy. He was indeed proving a wonder horse.

And so it continued when he was six years old, in 1770. During the winter he had filled out and matured and, if anything, was even more impressive – on those occasions when any horse dared to take him on. He was still considered something of an ugly duckling, and his conformation would not have won him classes in the show ring, but he had that most important quality of all: heart. In addition, he possessed 'speed, stride, ability to carry weight, strength of wind and power of endurance never surpassed, if equalled'.[3]

---

3   Theo Taunton, *Famous Horses: With Portraits Pedigrees, Principal Performances, Descriptions of Races and Various Interesting Items Extending over a Period of Nearly Two Centuries*, London, 1896.

Eclipse ran in better-class races this season, too, beginning at 'headquarters', Newmarket, on the Beacon Course (4 miles, 1 furlong, 138 yards) on 17 April. His jockey, as usual, let him run as he liked, which for one thing was with a very low head carriage and for another quite often looked as if he was running away. Maybe he was! None of his opponents was ever once able to 'make a race of it'.

Two days later, Dennis O'Kelly appeared on the card for the first time as the owner of Eclipse. This was over the round course, 4 miles, and Eclipse's opponents were Diana, Pensioner and Chigger, finishing in that order behind him. However, although they were not 'distanced', both Diana and Chigger were withdrawn from the second heat, leaving Pensioner to follow in his wake, a distance behind.

Eclipse had a break before reappearing in Guildford in June (walkover), Nottingham in July (walkover) and York in August (walkover). When he came up against real rivals three days later, still in York, he had not actually run a race since April. It made no difference. At odds of 1–20 (and 1–100 in running, so betting in running is not a new practice), he beat Tortoise and Bellario. At Lincoln in September he again walked over, and so it was on to Newmarket in October for a two-day meeting. When he beat Corsican, owned by Sir Charles Bunbury, at odds of 1–70 it was to be his last race. No one turned out the next day to take him on, so his final 'race' became another walkover. He had won all eighteen of his races as he liked – albeit that eight of them were walkovers. He was never once pushed out, and he certainly never felt the whip.

While a select few others in history have been able to match his race record, it is at stud that Eclipse became immortalised. He sired an astonishing 862 winners, and today over 90 per cent of Thoroughbreds trace to him in their tail male line. Eclipse sired three of the first five Derby winners, two of them owned by Dennis O'Kelly: in 1781, the appropriately named Young Eclipse and in 1874, Sergeant. In 1783, Saltram won for Mr Parker. Eclipse also soon proved that he could sire offspring well adapted to the new shorter races for younger horses.

After his death from colic at the age of twenty-four, Eclipse was dissected to try to work out the secret of his success. He literally had 'a big heart'. It was found to weigh 14 pounds, more than twice the normal weight of horses' hearts of that era, which was approximately 6 pounds. Eclipse's huge heart pumped blood around his body more effectively, while his back legs gave plenty of leverage. Powerful lungs completed the winning combination. Today, the normal weight of a horse's heart is 8.5 pounds. American Triple Crown winner Secretariat's heart was estimated at 22 pounds, and Phar Lap, 1930 Melbourne Cup winner, was found to be twice the average.

The skeleton of Eclipse is on permanent display in the National Horse Racing Museum, Newmarket (loaned from the Royal Veterinary College). In July 2011, an epic Coral–Eclipse Stakes at Sandown was won by the Australian 'wonder horse' So You Think from the previous year's Derby and Arc winner Workforce. Dual Oaks winner Snow Fairy was also in the field. The 1-mile-2-furlong event was founded in honour of Eclipse in 1886 when the winner was Bendigo. (Coral, the bookmakers, is the oldest current horse-racing sponsor in Britain, having started in 1976.) When the race was founded, the £10,000 in prize money was the biggest anywhere – and more than twice that of the Derby. Traditionally, the 'Eclipse' is the first race when the current year's classic three-year-olds take on their elders. As it is run over a longer distance than the Guineas and a shorter one than the Derby, it sometimes attracts the winners of one or the other. Or, as in the case of Sea The Stars, both. Sea The Stars, not surprisingly, descends from Eclipse on both sides of his pedigree.

3

Bend Or

B end Or was bred by the 1st Duke of Westminster at Eaton
Stud, Cheshire – home in the mid twentieth century of
Arkle's owner, Anne, Duchess of Westminster. Bend Or
grew to be a large stallion but was noted for his unusual docility.
He was sired by Doncaster, a son of Stockwell, out of Rouge Rose,
a mare by Thormanby, who won the 1860 Epsom Derby and the
1861 Ascot Gold Cup and who was, in 1869, the leading sire in
Great Britain and Ireland.

Bend Or's name comes from the heraldry term for 'a bend
which is golden or yellow in colour'. Looking at a picture, it shows
a much more 'modern' horse than in the first century of the

Thoroughbred (though perhaps that is due more to the dawn of photography versus the greater 'poetic licence' of earlier artists). A chestnut, he had some white on all four legs. He was compact, with good bone (that is, the bone between the knee and the fetlock was dense and strong) and lovely conformation. Unusually, he was spotted, with white flecks on his chestnut coat, and, like his dam-sire Thormanby, he had black spots on his neck, shoulder and quarters. Apparently he also had a model temperament.

In the summer of 2012, DNA samples taken from the skeleton of Bend Or, housed in the Natural History Museum, London, proved conclusively that he was, in fact, another chestnut by Doncaster called Tadcaster born on the same estate and in the same year; the two colts had been switched inadvertently as yearlings. A stewards' enquiry was held after he won the Derby, finding in Bend Or's favour. I will continue to call him Bend Or rather than Tadcaster, as that is how he is remembered.

Of all the many star horses and jockeys through the centuries, there comes every now and again a man or a horse destined for megastardom. Eclipse, Nijinsky, Arkle and Sea The Stars are equine examples, and Fred Archer, Steve Donoghue, Sir Gordon Richards, Lester Piggott and Tony McCoy are among the humans. 'Heart' coupled with innate ability singles out the horses while probably the biggest single factor among the men is ambition coupled with hard work. The driving force behind Fred Archer and Tony McCoy, for instance, was similar: sheer determination, hard work and the ever-present will to win, be it humble selling race, classic or championship.

In basic statistics, Fred Archer won the jockeys flat championship, for the rider with the most wins in one year, for thirteen consecutive years, before shooting himself dead at the age of twenty-nine following the death of his beloved wife in childbirth with their daughter. Tony McCoy, by happy contrast, collected his OBE from the Queen in June 2011, accompanied by his wife and adored daughter and has won seventeen consecutive jump jockeys titles. Both men were tall for race-riding which resulted in constant 'wasting' in order to do the required weight, and both broke many riding records – the popular 'A.P.' McCoy continues to do so.

Fred Archer rode 2,748 winners from 8,084 starts. In 1885 he rode 246 winners, a record that wasn't broken until Gordon Richards' 1933 tally of 269. He won the Epsom Derby five times and a total of twenty-one classic races.

In 2002, Tony McCoy beat Gordon Richards' seasonal record by twenty, with 289 winners. In 2006 he became the first jump jockey to ride a career tally of 2,500 winners, and just three years later he surpassed even that when memorably, at the attractive Sussex track of Plumpton, nestled beneath the South Downs, he steered home his 3,000th. He has won the 'classic' National Hunt races of the Cheltenham Gold Cup, Champion Hurdle, Queen Mother Champion Chase, King George VI Chase and, finally, at his fifteenth attempt, the Grand National, and looks to be heading for 4,000 winners.

Fred Archer was born on Cleeve Hill, overlooking Cheltenham racecourse, and began his apprenticeship as a slip of a boy, eleven years of age, with the fastidious Matt Dawson in his Heath House, Newmarket, stables – now run equally meticulously by Sir Mark Prescott. In 1869, 100 years after Eclipse began racing, twelve-year-old Archer won his first race, a steeplechase at Bangor. Just four years later he was Champion Flat Jockey, a title he retained annually until his death. Blissfully married to his boss's niece, Helen Rose (Nellie) Dawson, he built Falmouth Lodge (now Pegasus Stables), Newmarket, in honour of his principal owner.

Archer rode many horses that would compare equally with modern heroes. However, he was racing at a time when, although racing was regulated, there were no such things as camera patrols or photo finishes. By all accounts, some of the races could be rough, and it is said that Archer could be as ruthless (and vocal) as any. If a young upstart tried to come up on his inside he was perfectly able to lift him over the rails. It is also said that he was a heavy gambler – although not always a successful one. Jockeys today are not allowed to bet – or to be paid for giving tips either.

A different era, but that does not detract from the quality of horses. Archer rode five Derby winners but without doubt the 'one that got away' was the superb unbeaten St Simon, who was not entered, and whose owner died before the race. Another old rule was that if, in the two years between entry and race, the owner of a Derby entry should die, the entry was nullified, and this was the case with St Simon – quite possibly the best horse not to have run in the Derby. (Today, in addition to being entered as a yearling, Derby prospects may also be entered, for a bigger fee, in the April before the June race, and then a third entry stage [called supplementary entry] for an even bigger fee, just five days before the race.)

By 1877, when Archer rode his first Derby winner, Silvio for Lord Falmouth, he was already the established champion jockey. The years 1880 and 1881 brought him Derby victories on Bend Or and the first American-bred winner Iroquois, followed in 1885 by Melton. Archer just got him up on the line in typically masterful fashion for owner the Marquis of Hastings. In 1886, Bend Or's son, Ormonde, was Archer's winner. Ormonde was a great tribute to his sire and suffered less from unsoundness. Ormonde won the Triple Crown and was also very popular with the racing public.

The story of Bend Or's Derby really begins the previous year, in 1879. For the horse himself it was straightforward enough: five runs as a two-year-old and five wins, including the Chesterfield Stakes, Richmond Stakes, Rous Memorial Stakes, and the Prince of Wales's Stakes (York). For his jockey, it was not so straightforward. Archer was breaking in one of Dawson's more difficult horses, Muley Edris – a colt as bad-tempered as Bend Or was kind. He had a savage tendency, biting and kicking out at anyone who came within his reach, and he was nearly impossible to ride, throwing mighty bucks and nasty rears. Fred's solution was to thrash him, and then to thrash him some more, exerting all his force and will on him. At last connections got him to a race, but still the colt was wilful, being difficult at the start, and trying to stop before the finish. Yet Fred forced him to win.

Fast forward to the spring of 1880, and Matt Dawson, Fred Archer and the whole stable were looking forward to Bend Or's attempt to win the Derby first time out. May Day morning dawned like any other for Archer: he was up at six and riding out first lot at 7 a.m. Morning prayers for the staff were led by the trainer in the little room at the end of his house, followed by tea, toast and then second lot. It was a beautiful morning, and Fred was looking forward to watching the Maypole dancing with Nellie and their friends later that evening.

As he was riding Muley Edris second lot, he took him out alone, even though he was more tractable those days, and the piece of work they did was perfectly satisfactory. At the end of the gallop, Archer slipped off the colt, and, looping the reins over his arm, he bent forward to open a gate. But Muley Edris had not forgotten the beatings of the year before. With Archer turned away from him, fiddling with the latch, the colt seized his moment, and, with mouth wide open, he grabbed Archer by the arm and savaged him, sinking his teeth into his flesh. Not content with that, he lifted the jockey off the ground and shook him like a rag doll. He carried the helpless man a few steps and dropped him. Worse was to come. He pinned his victim to the ground by kneeling with his front legs on his chest. Suddenly his back legs slipped, almost causing him to fall, and with that he loosened his grip and galloped away just as help for Archer arrived.

Archer's arm hung useless by his side, mutilated. He was stretchered to Heath House, and the doctor was called. The damage was more than his skills could cope with, and Nellie accompanied her husband to hospital. The great Fred Archer's career looked over.

Three weeks later, with the Derby approaching, the wound was not healing. Worse, from Fred's point of view, he was putting on weight. His principal patron, Lord Falmouth, despatched him by train to his surgeon in London.

Fred asked the famous surgeon, 'Will I be fit for the Derby?'

'I think you can go,' the surgeon said.

'Yes, but can I ride?'

'Better drive, my boy, better drive.'

Exasperated, Fred said, 'Do you know who I am? I am in my profession what you are in yours.' He explained that he wanted to win the Derby on Bend Or. The surgeon asked Fred how much money he would lose if he was unable to take the ride.

'About £2,000.'

'Well,' the surgeon said, 'I wish my profession were half as profitable as yours!'

The doctor strapped Archer up, but the arm still failed to respond. Time was running out, and Fred became depressed, believing he was finished. He was nervy, highly strung and irascible – he bad-mouthed anyone unfortunate enough to be within earshot. In his attempt to lose weight, he purged himself more drastically than ever.

Archer then went to a bonesetter who strapped an iron rod to his arm, enabling him to ride out. Matt Dawson and Bend Or's owner, the Duke of Westminster, courageously agreed to allow him to ride in the Derby. He now had a matter of days in which to lose a stone in weight and regain his fitness – but his downheartedness was replaced by confidence: Bend Or was up against a good horse in Robert the Devil – and Fred was bullish about beating him. Just as he prepared himself there arose doubts about the horse. Bend Or was suffering from sore shins. His trainer, Robert Peck, spent the night before the Derby rubbing brandy into the chestnut's front shins to try and strengthen them and to get the blood circulating in the affected part to reduce the soreness which could make him lame.

Early on Derby Day the Downs were already thronging with people. Gypsies were selling lucky heather and telling fortunes, and card sharks were raking in gamblers' money.

Archer walked the course. As always he planned to stay on the inside. He left the gaiety behind him and headed towards the grandstand where the swells wore top hats and tails and the women beautiful dresses and hats. Behind the stands, rows of fine carriages were lined up. Archer headed for the weighing room and sat himself on the scales.

In the stables, Peck rubbed more brandy into Bend Or's legs. He hoped the fragile legs would be able to cope with the contours and gradients of the track.

At last they were all in the parade ring, and Fred was legged up into the saddle, the cloth beneath it showing the number 7. He cantered to the start and secured his usual inside berth. His white face glowered at any jockey who tried to get near him, and he issued dire threats to those who dared.

The white flag dropped. Fred exploded, swearing at those around him, threatening to put anyone over the rails who might try to steal that position from him, demanding he be given room. Now the horses were galloping flat out towards Tattenham Corner.

Bend Or was 'feely' (his jockey could sense the horse was feeling a bit sore) coming down the Hill, and others crowded in on him. Suddenly he was in danger of losing his place. Then he lost a shoe (just as the Queen's Carlton House was to at a crucial stage of the 2011 Derby). Now everyone was cursing, Archer most fiercely of all. He was so close to the rails that he had to lift his left leg to prevent it being scraped. Robert the Devil had secured a long lead and was scooting for home; he looked unbeatable.

The track was now level, and Bend Or regained his balance. With only one arm working properly, Fred propelled his mount along with all the rest of his strength from his legs and one arm. The gap was closing.

The winning post was nearing. It was 100 yards away. Fred went for his whip with his injured arm and dropped it. They were getting closer. The leader's jockey, hearing them, looked round – it unbalanced his horse. In that moment Fred and Bend Or made one final effort. The two horses passed the post locked together. No one knew who had won.

In the paddock, Peck and the Duke looked at each other questioningly. The number-board man climbed into position . . . and posted number 7 the winner, by a head.

The crowds erupted, and the cheering lasted for minutes. They mobbed Archer as their adored hero rode in. Some of them booed the loser, chanting that he'd thrown the race away. Archer magnanimously shouted, 'That isn't true, the lad rode as well as any lad could but met a better horse.' To a reporter, he admitted with masterly understatement, 'It was not wise of him, perhaps, to look round.'

It was truly one of the greatest rides ever given by any jockey down through the centuries. Fred Archer himself considered Bend Or possibly the best horse he ever rode. He ran four more times as a three-year-old but was plagued by the shin problem, and Robert the Devil won three of them. Bend Or won next time out after the Derby, taking the St James's Palace Stakes at Royal Ascot, but he was unable to run again until the St Leger in September. He finished only fifth in this to Robert the Devil and was then second to him in both the Great Foal Stakes and in the Champion Stakes.

He redeemed himself once more when he reappeared as a four-year-old, winning the 1881 City and Suburban Handicap at

Epsom Downs and then beating his archrival Robert the Devil in the Epsom Gold Cup. He also won the Champion Stakes that year before the problem of sore shins returned. Carrying top weight (and 8 pounds more than the next weighted horse), he was not disgraced in finishing fifth in the Cambridgeshire Handicap.

Bend Or retired to stud, the winner of ten of his fourteen races, and he also became a good sire. He passed on his spotted coat to some of his progeny, and also his wonderfully placid, docile temperament. In both 1901 and 1902 he was leading broodmare sire in Britain and Ireland, and he was the dam-sire of Sceptre, winner of four classics in 1902. His descendants included Phar Lap and The Tetrarch, who carried some of Bend Or's unusual spots in his coat and was voted Britain's two-year-old of the twentieth century. Without doubt his most famous son was Triple Crown winner Ormonde. He also sired 2,000 Guineas winner Bona Vista.

Bend Or died aged twenty-six in 1903, the year the Wright brothers patented their aeroplane and a fifteen-year-old horse called Manifesto, carrying 12 stone 3 pounds, finished third in the Grand National.

4

Manifesto

When Fred Archer died so tragically in 1886, the pinnacle of steeplechasing was the Grand National at Aintree, a handicap in which luck has always played a part due to the awesome fences and long distance. The first winner in 1839 was the aptly named Lottery, and Archer's father, William, had won on Little Charley in 1858. Two years after Archer's death, in 1888, one of the all-time Grand National greats, Manifesto, was born on an estate near Kells, Co. Meath.

The Cheltenham Gold Cup was not founded until 1924, when it was won by Red Splash, and it was probably post-war when, as a level-weighted contest (like the Derby) it took over the mantle of blue riband (highest honour attainable) from its great handicap rival. It is the Grand National, nevertheless, that has remained the world's most famous steeplechase.

Without exception, every year throws up a good story, quite often a fairytale, and there have been some outstanding winners over the 170 years. Of the seven individual horses who have won the Aintree race more than once, Red Rum is the only three-times winner. Manifesto broke a number of records: most runs in the race (eight), joint highest winning weight of 12 stone 7 pounds and highest placed weight of 12 stone 13 pounds. He was also third three times. Between his two wins he was hot favourite in 1898, but was unable to run.

Manifesto's breeder was Protestant landowner Harry Dyas, who had a 4,000-acre estate near Kells, Co. Meath. He was known as a wild character and, for a long time, a highly eligible bachelor. He was also a terrific shot and in 1876 went to America for the centennial long-range rifle-shooting championships where he was a member of the winning team. 'He was the best shot in the world at 1,000 yards,' his grandson Kim Dyas told me, adding, 'To think, here we are well into the twenty-first century talking about my nineteenth-century Victorian grandfather!'

Late in life, Dyas married Hilda O'Brien, a twenty-one-year-old convent-educated girl. He died two years later, leaving her with a two-year-old daughter, Laura. Laura is still alive, aged ninety-seven, although suffering with advanced dementia. She had three sons, the youngest of whom, Kim, was born when she was forty.

Manifesto's sire was Man of War (by Ben Battle), often confused with the American sire Man O' War (born in 1917), out of a mare called Vae Victis ('woe to the vanquished') by King Victor. Man of War was by Ben Battle out of Wisdom, and Ben Battle was out of Young Alice. Her grandsire was Melbourne (he appears in both sides of the pedigree). Melbourne was also grandsire of Ascetic, who in turn sired three Grand National winners: Cloister (1893), Drumcree (1903) and Ascetic's Silver (1906).

Harry Dyas's home-bred mare Gentle Ida was also by Man of War, and Harry Dyas originally rated her more highly than Manifesto. One can also assume from her name that she was of a better temperament than Man of War, who could better have been named 'Man Eater'. He was so savage that Harry Dyas used to lay bets with visitors that they couldn't get the better of him. Dyas would mention the nature of the beast, and the visitor, believing himself to be what today is called a horse whisperer, would willingly take on the bet. When they reached Man of War's stable, the volunteer would not be so willing to venture in as the stallion paced up and down, teeth bared, eyes flashing, tail swishing. Most conceded defeat without even trying to enter.

Before turning his attention to stallion duties he had been a useful enough racehorse, winning several flat races as a three-year-old in Ireland, but he failed to follow up that form in similar events in England. He was switched to hurdling there, winning nine hurdle races before retiring back to Meath to stand at stud.

Manifesto was a bright bay built in the mould of a model steeplechaser: well proportioned with good shoulders (that would help him carry the huge weights allotted to him), powerful quarters, good bones and a class head with a white star between his kind eyes.

He was also a gawky, unfurnished youngster, and Harry Dyas, to his credit, gave him plenty of time before facing him with the Aintree challenge. Before 1880 there had been four five-year-old winners of the Grand National, whereas Manifesto did not run in the race until he was seven years old. Today that is the minimum age allowed, and very few seven-year-olds are entered, let alone run.

However, Manifesto did begin his racing career as a four-year-old, getting off to an inauspicious start when he fell in a chase at Manchester. A month later he reappeared at the same course, this time in a hurdle race, and he won, earning £39 in prize money for his owner. He ran twice more, and then, impressing many racegoers, he won the Irish Champion Steeplechase at Leopardstown. This was a portent of the talent to come, and after it he returned to the Dyas's Meath estate to be given more time to mature while roaming the well-grassed acres.

Harry Dyas kept the bay to a light programme over the next couple of years. Two runs as a five-year-old brought a win in Derby, and at six years of age, in 1894, the year that the Manchester Ship Canal was opened, he won the Lancashire Chase at Manchester. This win resulted in him catching the eye not only of the public and also of the handicapper, who allotted the gelding 11 stones 2 pounds for his first attempt at the Grand National in spring 1895.

On the morning of 29 March 1895, a dense fog hung over the Grand National course and the ground was heavy. Spectators could barely see, and the jockeys could only see each fence as it loomed out of the murk and the mud. Terry Kavanagh was Manifesto's jockey, and he soon found his mount adapting to the mighty fences, perhaps because Harry Dyas had built replicas of the Aintree fences at home. He was surrounded by eighteen good horses including two previous winners, Father O'Flynn (1892) and Why Not (1894), as well as the runner-up in the intervening year, Aesop. This horse had been second in 1893 to one of the National greats, Cloister, a magnificent animal, and on the strength of that (and ignoring his fifth placing behind Why Not) Aesop was now sent off the 5–1 favourite. It is curious to note that while Why Not had been 5–1 joint favourite when he won, he was now, one year later, starting at an extraordinary 50–1. In the event, it was Wild Man from Borneo, third the previous year at 40–1, who took the honours at a price of 10–1, ahead of Cathal and Van Der Berg, with Manifesto, carrying more weight than those three, a creditable fourth.

The following year, on 26 March, Manifesto was allotted 11 stones 4 pounds. His Grand National followed a run where he finished unplaced in the Midland Chase at Nottingham and had a walkover for a race in Manchester that netted £98 for his owner. The prize money for the Grand National had jumped dramatically from £1,500 to £2,500, plus entrance stakes. The bottom weight had been reduced to 9 stone 7 pounds, from which two of the twenty-eight starters ran (one of them a pound overweight).

The weather was much better than at the previous year's meeting. Father O'Flynn, Why Not, Wild Man from Borneo (at an astonishing price of 40–1), Cathal and Van Der Berg were all in it again, but a newcomer, Rory O'More, was favourite, and another newcomer, The Soarer, won it. His rider, Mr D. Campbell, had made his reconnaissance of the course with military precision. (A subaltern with the 9th Lancers, he was later to become General Sir David Campbell.) Shortly before the race he had sold the horse to Mr W. H. Walker, who in later years became Lord Wavertree, founder of the Japanese Gardens and a fine stud in Co. Kildare that in due course would become the Irish National Stud. His father, a former Mayor of Liverpool, founded the Walker Gallery.

As for Manifesto, he joined the long list in the race's history of first-fence fallers, though whether he was brought down by Redhill, or Redhill by him, or the two collided in mid-air causing both to fall, has remained a matter of debate down the ages. Whatever happened, his jockey John Gourley found himself on the ground ignominiously early.

It was to be a case of third time lucky for Manifesto in 1897, although Harry Dyas let it be known that he fancied his home-bred mare, Gentle Ida, more. In fact, he tried to sell both horses in advance of the race, something that is not unusual in the run-up when there might be one or two people eager to become owners of a Grand National runner, especially if it is one seen to have a good chance – for which the owner can then ask an inflated price. Harry Dyas told his agent Tom Vigors that he thought one of his pair would win; each had the then-enormous price tag of £5,000, and neither found a buyer.

Harry Dyas sent Manifesto to be trained in England before the race. The reason is unclear, but it may have been so that the horse did not have to keep crossing the Irish Sea for his races. Horses have travelled by sea since ancient times, often for reasons of warfare, but a racehorse which has had a long and perhaps rough sea crossing is bound to be at a disadvantage with those trained 'at home'. Other means of horse transport were improving at this time, mainly with the arrival of the 'iron horse', the railway system.

Eclipse and his fellow 'running horses' would have been walked between the various venues. Nearly a century later, in 1836, there was a great coup pulled off by Lord George Bentinck, founder of the Bentinck Benevolent Fund for flat race trainers and jockeys in times of need. Lord Lichfield's horse, Elis, had been entered for the Doncaster St Leger but it was publicly known that the horse was in Goodwood, Sussex, some 200 miles away, so it was 'impossible' for him to get there in time to run. Lord Bentinck masterminded a plan of which he was so certain that he wagered a bet of £1,000 on Elis at 12–1 for the St Leger. He commissioned the building of a padded wooden box on wheels, into which Elis was loaded and then conveyed to Doncaster. A team of six carriage horses was changed daily, and Elis arrived fresh, duly winning the St Leger – and those few 'in the know' their handsome bets.

Well in advance of the National, Manifesto arrived into the stables at Everleigh, Wiltshire, owned by Willie McAuliffe and set in the glorious expanse of Salisbury Plain. Today the stables form the second yard of royal trainer Richard Hannon and his son Richard Jr., and, as in Manifesto's day, horses can leave their stable in any direction in the morning and remain entirely on the centuries-old, springy turf of Salisbury Plain, which never gets either too hard or too wet. Their most frequent companions are hares, foxes and sheep, and overhead rooks caw and buzzards mew to add to the music of pounding hooves, horses' snorts, the jingling of snaffle bits and the banter of the lads and lasses riding them.

Manifesto thrived. The 1897 Grand National drew near, and he was raring to go. Terry Kavanagh was given the ride, and he intended to improve on his fourth of two years before. He got himself fit by humping sacks of potatoes, and he improvised a sauna, so the story goes, by sleeping in the manure heap. Shortly before the race, Gentle Ida was withdrawn, and nine-year-old Manifesto was left as favourite. It was the year of Queen Victoria's Golden Jubilee and there was a record crowd. They were aided by the addition for the first time of name cloths under the saddles of all twenty-eight runners. More to the point, they were treated to an epic race, in which Manifesto, on 11 stone 3 pounds, drew further and further ahead of his field. Only Timon could keep with him as far as the penultimate fence, where he fell, and when Cathal fell at the last Manifesto came home in splendid isolation, twenty lengths ahead of his nearest pursuer, to the appreciative cheers of the crowds.

He ran twice more that season, falling in the Lancashire Chase, but he won the end-of-season 3½-mile Grand International at Sandown, the forerunner of the Whitbread Gold Cup, now the Bet365 Chase.

Aintree looked his oyster, and Harry Dyas this time achieved the aim of selling Manifesto before the following year's race. The buyer was Mr J. G. Bulteel, who had made his fortune on the Stock Exchange, and he paid a huge sum of £4,000 for Manifesto. He sent him to W. H. (Willie) Moore, who trained for the licence-holder John Collins and who had already been successful in the 1894 Grand National with Why Not. Manifesto had won a 2-mile chase in Gatwick in February carrying 12 stone 10 pounds, giving a massive 37 pounds to the runner-up, and he was unsurprisingly favourite for the following month's National. Barely a week before the event, fit, eager and raring to go, Manifesto escaped from his stable, galloped free and, attempting to clear a five-barred gate, rapped a fetlock so badly that he was unable to run for nearly a year. The stable lad who had inadvertently left the stable door unlatched 'did a runner', the story goes, and turned up in another stable under an assumed name. The 1898 race brought compensation to jockey John Gourley for his previous first-fence fall with Manifesto when he won on Drogheda.

John Bulteel had to wait until 1899 to see his colours sported by Manifesto in the Grand National. The eleven-year-old was allotted top weight of 12 stone 7 pounds. This time Gentle Ida was in the race and carrying a stone less. Harry Dyas, himself a renowned betting man, was convinced that not even Manifesto could give the mare a stone – she was second top weight and started 4–1 favourite. Nothing and no one, least of all the weight, was going to stop Manifesto, even though he had to give as much as 3 stone to two of his eighteen rivals.

An error by the groundsmen nearly cost Manifesto the race. Hay had been strewn both sides of the fences ahead of the day because of frost – the race looked threatened by the cold spell at one stage – but the men had failed to remove one patch beyond the Canal Turn before the race. Ridden by George Williamson, Manifesto slipped on the hay, came down and slid along the ground on his belly. Williamson, to his eternal credit, sat quiet as a mouse, still astride the stricken horse, and so, as Manifesto regained his legs, his jockey was still in the saddle. The incident would have spelled the end of the race for many horses and jockeys, but Williamson neither unbalanced his horse nor harried him to make up the lost ground. There was still a long way to go, and the patience paid off.

For Gentle Ida it was not so good as she fell at Valentine's. She then proceeded to run loose stride for stride with Manifesto himself, the pair pulling clear of the remainder just as it might have panned out had she retained her jockey. She, too, incidentally, had been sold – for £5,000, even more than Manifesto. Her luckless new owner was Horatio Bottomley.

In gratitude for his horsemanship, Mr Bulteel, who is said to have won more than £10,000 in bets, gave George Williamson £2,800, the equivalent of the prize fund, in addition to his £100 retainer fee. By all accounts it was well deserved. And as for Manifesto, the crowds adored him, even trying to pull strands of hair from his tail as keepsakes. For his part, Manifesto knew he was king and wore his crown majestically.

Manifesto had now won the Grand National twice, this time with a joint weight-carrying record of 12 stones 7 pounds, yet it was in defeat the following year that he ran what was probably not only his finest race but one of the greatest races of all time. In 1900, the handicapper allotted Manifesto, now twelve years old, a welter 12 stone 13 pounds. It was too much, but he ran his heart out trying to prove it wasn't.

There was much attention on the Prince of Wales's horse, Ambush II, who had finished unplaced behind Manifesto the previous year at just five years of age. There were as many eyes for the heavily weighted, aging dual hero.

In the sixteen-runner race the favourite Hidden Mystery was brought down by the loose horse Covert Hack at the water jump in front of the stands. Covert Hack, a stable companion of Ambush II, had fallen at the first. With the favourite out of the race, Ambush II was up with the leaders but there, creeping ever closer on the second circuit, was Manifesto. As he cleared the Canal Turn the crowds gasped. Could he do it? And when he jumped into the lead two from home their cheers rose to a crescendo; he surely could do it. At the last fence, Ambush II passed him, yet even then, under 12 stone 13 pounds, Manifesto fought back, and for a stride or two passed him. There was only 100 yards to go. The royal runner Ambush II and the heavily burdened dual victor Manifesto duelled it out; with younger years and 24 pounds less weight, Ambush drew ahead, and George Williamson eased his hero, allowing another runner, Barsac, to just take second place by a neck.

There were, of course, hats off for the royal winner – but there were tears from grown men for the plucky Manifesto. It was without doubt one of the all-time great steeplechases, and for Manifesto it was one of the finest performances in defeat ever witnessed on a racecourse.

When Manifesto did not run the following year it was reasonable to suppose he had retired, but he ran in the Grand Nationals of 1902, 1903 and, incredibly, 1904, when he was sixteen years old. On that occasion, carrying 12 stone 1 pound, he jumped round safely and finished an honourable last to the New Zealand horse Moifaa, but in both 1902 (12 stone 8 pounds, at fourteen years of age) and 1903 (12 stone 3 pounds, at fifteen years of age) he finished third behind Shannon Lass and Drumcree respectively.

Manifesto's record in the Grand National is one that I am certain will never be broken.

Having been lucky enough to watch Arkle, Red Rum, Dawn Run and, in 2011, Long Run, I can say that Manifesto, along with Cloister and Troytown, are the horses from the past I would most like to have seen.

Manifesto's racing silks, as worn by Terry Kavanagh, along with the magnificent tall 1897 cup with staghead handles, were loaned to the Aintree Museum. Memorabilia sells well at auction – £4,000 for old papers about Manifesto, for example. His skeleton was sent to the Liverpool School of Veterinary Medicine where it was restored and is now in the University of Liverpool Museum. 'So Manny had another career for about a century,' Kim Dyas said.

5

Cottage Rake

C ottage Rake was bred by Richard Vaughan from Hunting Hall, Castletown Roche, Co. Cork, just a few miles from Vincent O'Brien's embryo training empire near Churchtown, Co. Cork. He was by Cottage (who went back to the great St Simon), who also sired Grand National winners Lovely Cottage (1946) and Sheila's Cottage (1948), one of only thirteen mares to win the great race.

Richard Vaughan's brother, Dr Otto Vaughan, a GP in Mallow, took over the ownership with the express intention of selling the horse on. He despatched the then five-year-old from the stable behind his surgery to Goffs Sales, in those days situated in

Ballsbridge (and a lively behind-the-scenes part of Dublin Horse Show week), but he failed to sell.

Vaughan brought him home, turned him out on the bog, and contacted the little local trainer to see if he would train him, again specifically to sell. Phonsie O'Brien, Vincent's capable amateur rider brother, collected him straight off the bog and led him off a pony and trap.

Not surprisingly, the horse was not only unfit but also unfurnished, and O'Brien wanted time to build him up. His owner wanted him on the racecourse, strutting his stuff, so in the end O'Brien entered him for a maiden hurdle and gave one of his stable staff the ride. The backward horse led from start to finish to win at 10–1. When he went on to win a bumper even more impressively, a good sale looked a foregone conclusion. Twice a sale fell through because Cottage Rake failed the veterinary examination for 'making a noise', that is, a problem with his wind. Dr Vaughan still wanted him sold and began enquiring about training costs in England.

Suddenly O'Brien realised he had better find a buyer himself if he wanted the clearly talented horse to remain in his yard. Mr Frank Vickerman, a wealthy wool merchant, had become his first owner only a couple of years before, sending him three horses – two of which, Dry Bob and Good Days, won both men plenty of money by landing the Autumn Double.

A deal was done, but Cottage Rake went lame, and the vet diagnosed rheumatism in his shoulder. O'Brien could not advise his buyer to go through with the sale, but Vickerman's first cheque in part payment had already been cashed by Vaughan, and to the doctor that meant the deal was irreversible. By one of those wonderful quirks of fate, Frank Vickerman was 'stuck' with Cottage Rake.

Despite his supposed problems, Cottage Rake continued his winning ways, adding to his initial two wins with another bumper and, in the autumn of 1946, the Naas November Handicap over 1½ miles. When Aubrey Brabazon first rode him in the 2½-mile Carrickmines Chase at Leopardstown, the bay with the white blaze already had a big reputation. Brabazon was injured and was not able to ride Cottage Rake again for a year, but they were to form such a close partnership that it is his name forever associated with that of the horse:

> Aubrey's up, the money's down
> The frightened bookies quake
> Come on me lads and give a cheer
> Begod 'tis Cottage Rake!

Although supposedly anonymous, Brabazon believed the writer of the ditty to be a particular person from North Cork. Aubrey Brabazon had a great philosophy of life which was to live it to the full, to leave the training to the trainer, to party wildly, drink copiously and tell great stories – and to take his 'day job' of race-riding deadly seriously. Out all night partying and drinking he might have been, but he would be sober and skilful in the saddle the next day. It is a spirit carried on by some of his cousins today.

Brabazon possessed what nowadays would be termed 'an old-fashioned seat', but he was seldom ejected from the saddle, as over a fence his lower legs were well forward, braced and ready to survive a blunder. He rode with quite long stirrups (but nothing like the almost straight leg of Fred Archer's day), the better to squeeze and urge a horse with, and had a long length of rein and lightness of touch that meant he seldom, if ever, interfered with a horse's mouth. He had seen the vicissitudes of the racing world at first hand as he grew up, with his father Cecil sometimes enjoying success (when the young Aubrey would find himself at a posh school) and others being on the floor (and it would be the local school, and helping with the chores in the yard before and after). There were a number of house moves, too, but once the family were installed in Rangers Lodge on the Curragh, that is where they stayed, and it was where Brabazon spent the rest of his life. I well remember listening to some of his reminiscences there in the kitchen, over a cup of tea (and doubtless a drop of the brown stuff poured into it) as we discussed a potential deal for a point-to-pointer. He became a successful bloodstock agent once he had 'hung up his racing boots'.

Cottage Rake had a distinctive racing style and not one that looked the most comfortable or would normally be associated with greatness. He was inclined to hold his head high and back a little, almost making it look as though he had a 'ewe neck'. And he wasn't always the most fluent of fencers in a steeplechase. He had abundant stamina (from his sire) and speed from his dam, Hartingo, who, it was said, wouldn't stay beyond 4 furlongs, let alone 3 miles!

By the time the 1947–8 season came around, Cottage Rake had won four chases the previous season as well as the Naas November Handicap and the 2-mile Irish Cesarewitch, both on the flat. O'Brien decided that, in spite of this, and although still a novice over fences, he would let Cottage Rake take his chance in the Cheltenham Gold Cup, no less. It was to be not only O'Brien's first runner in England but also his own first journey across the Irish Sea.

The story of Cottage Rake's first Gold Cup, and of the 'steadier' his jockey and trainer had before it, is told in Brabazon's evocative memoir, *Racing Through My Mind*:

> I had no more rides before the big race so I weighed out early. Vincent saddled the horse and then came back to me in the weigh room. The crowd had gone out to see the race before the Gold Cup so we were left to ourselves, looking at each other with nothing left to be said. I can't deny that I was a bit nervous just then – like a soldier in those last quiet moments before a great battle – and Vincent, a worrier at the best of times, was certainly no better.
>
> 'I'll tell you what we'll do Vincent,' I said, 'We'll go for one drink to calm the nerves.' So, with the bars virtually empty during the race we did just that. I can't think what the few onlookers must have thought of the Irish trainer and his jockey ordering two brandy and ports half an hour before the Gold Cup. To be honest, I don't think we attracted much attention. After all, I had only ridden a couple of winners in England, Vincent had yet to open his account, and our horse in the Gold Cup was a virtual novice who had fallen in his last race. Nobody in that bar was too bothered with us. But that one drink marked our last few moments of

anonymity. Unfortunately, we were unable to repeat the ritual in subsequent years!

The race got off to an eventful start. At the first fence the favourite, Cool Customer, fell. I had ridden Cool Customer to win five races when he was trained in Ireland by Tony Riddell-Martin. Subsequent events were to show that his early exit was a real stroke of luck for us. With about a mile to run the race was developing into a duel between Cottage Rake and Martin Moloney's mount, Happy Home. We were racing neck and neck from fence to fence. Happy Home, the experienced chaser who had finished second in the previous year's Gold Cup, was just edging it at the fences but Cottage Rake appeared to have the slight advantage between jumps.

As we thundered towards the last Martin had a slight advantage but I was still quietly confident. Often in a race I would find myself acting instinctively, only afterwards figuring out what I had done. But I remember that it was a conscious decision of mine to let Cottage Rake 'fiddle' the last fence. He was never a horse that you could ask to stand off at the wing and, anyhow, he was still a virtual novice. I figured that if we got safely over the last we could win the race on the flat. What I hadn't bargained for was Martin's magnificent performance on Happy Home. He drove him at the last like a demon and got a wonderful leap from the horse. They landed running while we brushed through

Plate 1   John Wootton's well-known portrait of the Byerley Turk. From Roger Longrigg, *The History of Horse Racing*, London: Macmillan, 1972, p. 59.

Plate 2   The unbeaten Eclipse, who also sired three of the first five Derby winners in the 1780s. The portrait is based on *Eclipse at New Market with Groom and Jockey* by George Stubbs.

Plate 3 In one of the sport's greatest riding feats, Fred Archer, with a badly injured arm, just gets Bend Or up to win the 1880 Epsom Derby from Robert the Devil. Archer had dropped his whip, but the picture shows him with one.

Plate 4 Manifesto, the magnificent winner of the Grand National in 1897 and 1899. From eight starts he was also third three times, fourth once and ninth at the age of sixteen.

Plate 5   One of the great Grand
          National winners, Manifesto,
          left, in action at Aintree. In
          the early days some of the
          Grand National fences were
          small, and the last two fences
          were sheep hurdles, as here.

Plate 6   Aubrey Brabazon, the
          Irish jockey who won the
          Cheltenham Gold Cup with
          Cottage Rake in 1948, 1949
          and 1950 and who won the
          Champion Hurdle twice on
          Hatton's Grace in 1949 and
          1950.

Plate 7   Cottage Rake, ridden by
          Aubrey Brabazon, winner of
          the Gold Cup.

Plate 8   American jockey Tommy Smith of Virginia rides Jay Trump during exercise at Lambourn, Berkshire, on 18 March 1965. They won the Grand National at Aintree nine days later.

Plate 9   Jay Trump (right), Tommy Smith up, passes the post to win the Grand National from the Scottish-trained Freddie (left), Pat McCarran up.

Plate 10 Nijinsky, ridden by Lester Piggott, storms clear of Gyr to win the Derby, 3 June 1970.

Plate 11 Irish racehorse trainer Vincent O'Brien with Nijinsky in the background, circa 1970.

Plate 12   On the bit and with springs in his heels, Golden Cygnet looked set for a glittering career. Here he is winning the 1978 Waterford Crystal Novices' Hurdle, Cheltenham, ridden by Niall Madden.

Plate 13   Istabraq with Charlie Swan winning his third consecutive Champion Hurdle at Cheltenham, March 2000.

Plate 14 (right)
Charlie Swan and Istabraq ride
victoriously into the winner's enclosure
after their third consecutive Smurfit
Champion Hurdle at Cheltenham.

Plate 15 (below)
Is something amiss? Istabraq and Charlie
Swan trail the field as they jump the
second flight and are about to pull up in
the Champion Hurdle in 2002.

Plate 16 Istabraq's connections, including trainer Aidan O'Brien, his wife Anne-Marie, jockey (now trainer) Charlie Swan, owner J. P. McManus, and the artist Nicola Russell at the unveiling of her painting at the 2011 Punchestown Festival.

the top of the fence. It must have looked all over at that crucial stage, and if I didn't have a truly great horse under me it would have been. As I gathered up Cottage Rake and set off in pursuit up the hill it seemed hopeless. But it is only under pressure that great horses reveal their true qualities. As I asked the big question the Rake responded with a turn of foot that was simply breathtaking. I got to Happy Home fifty yards from the line and won going away by a length and a half.

I saw an old newsreel film of the finish for the first time a few years ago, and the only other time that I saw such speed at the end of a long distance chase was when Arkle beat Mill House in their famous 1964 encounter.[1]

Martin Moloney's riding performance is worth mentioning here, for often a jockey is praised for winning rides and forgotten (or berated) for losing ones. The way in which he drove Happy Home into the last fence, gaining a good length over his rival in mid-air, was both brave and inspiring, and Martin himself rated it one of his finest riding performances, for all that it ended in defeat.

Cottage Rake was welcomed home to Co. Cork with bonfires and celebrations but O'Brien had cause for concern. Frank Vickerman was contemplating selling his star, and in his proposed purchaser, Dorothy Paget, there was a seemingly bottomless purse. She won the Cheltenham Gold Cup five times with Golden Miller and once each with Roman Hackle and Mont Tremblant, but her Happy Home had now finished runner-up twice.

---

1   Aubrey Brabazon, *Racing Through My Mind*, Vota Books, pp. 75–7.

Whatever was or wasn't going on behind the scenes, Cottage Rake remained with his current owner and trainer. After his summer break he recorded a facile win in a 3-mile chase at Limerick Junction (now Tipperary), putting up a perfect performance and proclaiming to the racing world that he was ready to defend chasing's crown. He had more to prove and a tougher job in the Emblem Chase at Manchester in November 1948 when Brabazon found himself once more upsides his old friend and rival, Martin Moloney, who this time was riding Lord Bicester's Silver Fame, the horse who still holds the record for the number of wins at Cheltenham (eleven).

Cottage Rake had to give 5 pounds to Silver Fame and a stone to Cromwell, Lord Mildmay's horse who had been so unlucky not to win the previous year's Grand National when the rider suffered neck cramp when in a commanding lead after the Canal Turn, finishing third in spite of all. The Emblem Chase proved a two-horse race as Cottage Rake and Silver Fame raced neck and neck towards the last, where the Rake once again made a mistake and Brabazon lost his whip. Luckily, this was an accessory not needed for Cottage Rake who, responding to his jockey's urgings with hands and heels, made up the two-length deficit and got up to win by a neck, once more showing his courage in a battle.

There followed no less a race than the King George VI Chase at Kempton on Boxing Day. Cottage Rake was up against Roimond, the second of Lord Bicester's two top-class horses of the time. A much flatter track than Cheltenham, the two courses can suit different types of horses, but to a good horse they come just the same. So it was with Cottage Rake who put up a first-rate performance, jumped fluently past Roimond in mid-air at the last fence and strode clear for a five-length victory.

Naturally, Cottage Rake was a warm favourite for the Cheltenham Gold Cup in March, but fears grew that he wouldn't make it due to a cough and a 'snotty' nose – not good at any time, but for a horse who might have a wind problem it could be career-ending should he run when the slightest trace remained.

We have seen that horses have since ancient times travelled by sea, that the early racehorses were walked between meetings, that a padded horse-drawn horsebox was introduced in 1836, and that by Manifesto's time steam trains had greatly improved the transport of horses. Now, in 1949, and this time with three horses to run at the Cheltenham Festival, the thirty-one-year-old O'Brien broke new ground by chartering an aeroplane, a former RAF transport plane, to convey his posse across the Irish Sea.

The three horses were Castledermot (for the 4-mile National Hunt Chase for amateur riders), Hatton's Grace (for the Champion Hurdle) and Cottage Rake, who got upset enough on the flight to alarm his stable lads.

Brabazon found himself duelling once again with Martin Moloney, who was on the current holder and dual victor of the Champion Hurdle, National Spirit. Hatton's Grace was making his debut attempt at the hurdling crown at the advanced age of nine – and he galloped away to score from National Spirit by six lengths. Hatton's Grace was also to win the Champion Hurdle for the next two years, becoming its first triple winner. Lord Mildmay on Castledermot followed up the next day in equally impressive fashion in the 4-mile amateurs chase.

Now, on the third and final day, it was down to Cottage Rake. How much had the hold-up in his work caused by his cold affected him? We shall never know, for, on Gold Cup morning, Prestbury Park, home of Cheltenham racecourse, was covered with a frost so hard it was too dangerous to race. The Cheltenham Gold Cup was postponed until April – by which time there were no doubts about Cottage Rake's well-being.

In the interim, Brabazon had married Ethne Dwyer and had to cut short their honeymoon to return for the rescheduled Gold Cup. He flew to Cheltenham and spent dinner the evening before the big race being lectured by Vickerman on exactly how he should ride the horse next day. Not surprisingly, Brabazon would have been 'far happier spending the evening with my new bride trying to forget for a few hours the big event the next day'.[2]

After dinner, the owner saw the jockey and his new wife safely into a taxi for an early night. Brabazon recalls:

> At this stage I have to admit to my shame that the pent-up tension within me came to bursting point and as Mr Vickerman closed the taxi door I let down the window to thank him for the evening. As the taxi was pulling away I couldn't resist adding ' . . . and with a bit of luck, Mr Vickerman, we're sure to be in the first three tomorrow.' As the Rake was odds-on favourite in a field of six, this cruel parting shot nearly finished the poor man.[3]

2   Brabazon, *Racing Through My Mind*, p. 87.
3   Brabazon, *Racing Through My Mind*, p. 88.

The race was no pushover. One of the contestants was Cool Customer, first-fence faller the previous year but winner of four chases since. Before he was sold to England, Brabazon had ridden him to five wins in Ireland, over 2 to 2½ miles. He knew he was up against a tough opponent – but he did wonder about his stamina. In the race, Cool Customer set out on the final circuit jumping and galloping fluently in the lead. Brabazon takes up the story:

Coolie got properly into his stride and put it up to the rest of us [. . .] the further we went the more I worried that he would be a hard nut to crack. I was niggling at the Rake as we approached the top of the hill. Turning into the straight I was under pressure and coming to the last I was a length behind and in serious trouble [. . .] the Rake didn't help matters by brushing the top of the last. We'd had a battle on our hands at this point the previous year, but now it was even tougher. This was not a question of timing a finishing burst, as I felt that the Rake was already flat out and not finding enough. I rode him up the hill as hard as ever I rode and the game old horse was giving his all. We clawed our way back up to the equally gallant 'Coolie,' and when the Rake found that bit to get to a horse on the run to the line he always seemed to find that little bit extra to go by. We won our second Gold Cup by two lengths after the hardest battle ever for horse – and rider! Cool Customer was a hell of a horse and he was probably at his very best that day. I believe it was the

superior stamina that won it for us. We wore down
Cool Customer in '49 whereas we had beaten Happy
Home for speed in '48.[4]

This time, quite rightly, Cottage Rake did not contest the Irish
Grand National or any other race for that matter. Instead, he went
off for a well-deserved rest and the summer at grass, while his
human connections, naturally, celebrated his success. It was this
victory that really started the now-traditional Irish–English rivalry
at the Cheltenham Festival and the tradition also of euphoric
scenes of Irish men (and women) in the winner's enclosure that
have become so much a part of the Cheltenham scene.

As the new decade dawned, Cottage Rake set out to defend
his Cheltenham crown. This time he did not go into the race
undefeated. After winning his usual race at Limerick Junction and
then one in Sandown, he was beaten on Boxing Day. In a great
duel, Dick Francis on Finnure got 'first run' in the King George at
Kempton and held on by three-quarters of a length, compensation
for Lord Bicester at last. Brabazon was out with a broken collar-
bone when Cottage Rake had the misfortune to be brought down
at Leopardstown.

Nevertheless, he was still favourite for the 1950 Gold Cup.
On the first day of the National Hunt Festival, Brabazon recorded
Champion Hurdle number two on Hatton's Grace. Two days of
lying low, being abstemious and having early nights before his and
Cottage Rake's date with destiny on day three were certainly not
his style.

---

4   Brabazon, *Racing Through My Mind*, p. 89.

These were the days when Vincent O'Brien was still training out of Churchtown before his move to Ballydoyle, and just about all of Cork, it seemed, had travelled to Cheltenham to watch 'their' horse run. Many of them planned to pull a strand of hair out of his tail if they could.

There were only five runners, and probably only Finnure could reasonably be mentioned in the same breath as the Rake. Martin Moloney was once again his main rival, and he did his best to execute a cunning plan designed to blunt Cottage Rake's finishing speed – but it was to no effect. Brabazon took hold of the race, unusually, on the top bend and stole it there. Probably the most famous picture of the Brab and the Rake is the one taken over the last fence where Brabazon has allowed himself a satisfied smile. He described the manoeuvre thus:

> It was clear that someone had to move soon. We were still only cantering, but the tension was building steadily, and by now Cottage Rake and Finnure were like two coiled springs. [. . .] In a split second, in what I can only describe as divine intervention, I decided to go *on* the bend. [. . .] No experienced rider ever asks a horse to accelerate on a bend.
>
> [. . .] The Rake responded to my unorthodox move in great style. We charged down the hill at a ferocious rate and came to the third last at sprinting pace [a fence notorious for falls]. If we had met it wrong I think they would still be digging us out of the Prestbury Park turf, but the gods were smiling on us

that day and we flew that crucial fence. In that instant
the race was won.[5]

The pair of them scorched to a ten-length victory. No wonder
there was a smile on Brabazon's face.

It was to prove Cottage Rake's last win. That season, he did
go on to contest the Irish Grand National again, and, carrying
12 stone 7 pounds, he finished fourth to Dominicks Bar (Martin
Moloney). Even then his season was not finished, and he was to
contest the Galway Plate in July. He finished fifth, giving nearly 3
stone to all four horses ahead of him. At last he was turned out for
his deserved summer holiday at grass.

Ironically, this horse with 'legs of iron', who had withstood all
those top races, met with a mishap. Accidents can and do happen
at grass, but the inestimable advantage of a summer break on 'Dr
Green' generally speaking outweighs the risk of accident. In fact,
turning Nijinsky out to grass at a time when he was the most valuable piece of horseflesh on earth did him so much good that once
back in work he was far more settled and never reared again. No
matter how well fenced or how large the field, it can happen that a
horse will gallop into a fence and get staked or fall while galloping
about and break a leg or strain a tendon.

One morning the cattle were still in the field when Cottage
Rake and his donkey companion were turned out. The donkey
wandered in among the cattle, and Cottage Rake 'lost' (couldn't
see) him, causing him to panic and gallop about so badly that he
strained a tendon. It meant a year off, and the only surprise was

---

5   Brabazon, *Racing Through My Mind*, pp. 98–9.

that he was not retired but raced again, at the age of thirteen. Brabazon rode him in his comeback race at the Leopardstown Christmas meeting, but they were a distant third behind, of all horses, Hatton's Grace. The upshot was that Cottage Rake's owner took him away from the trainer – no matter that Vincent O'Brien had trained him to win three Cheltenham Gold Cups – and sent him to Gerald Balding near Andover, Hampshire.

Brabazon, on the point of retirement, rode the fourteen-year-old in a chase at Hurst Park. The old horse couldn't stride out in his old way on the firm ground and fell at the last open ditch. He was uninjured, but the Brab broke an arm. Cottage Rake went on running until he was fifteen years old, without success. I'm sure readers must be screaming as loudly as I am, 'if only he had been retired earlier.' After such an honourable career he most certainly owed nothing to anybody, and tender loving care in his old age was the least he deserved. He occasionally paraded for the public once he was retired and died aged twenty-two in 1961.

6

Jay Trump

The fresh young Thoroughbred spooked at an imaginary heeby-jeeby man and jinked suddenly sideways – as they do. His rider, being the horseman that he was, made the horse go back and pass the bogey spot again. Normally, that is all that is required to soothe a horse, to show it that there's nothing to fear and to restore its confidence. In future, it should pass the spot without so much as blinking an eye. Not this horse. Not only did he spook again, but also, and much worse, he comprehensively dumped his rider, who hit the ground in such a way that he was paralysed instantly. (There but for the grace of God go so many of us.) For Crompton (Tommy) Smith, the jockey who won the

Aintree Grand National and three Maryland Hunt Cups on Jay Trump, it would mean the rest of his life in bed. He would never walk again.

I visited him on a 'good day' when I was over for the 2010 Maryland Hunt Cup. In the third week of April Tommy Smith can always expect a few extra visitors, and when the visitor is to be a first-time rider in the formidable Maryland Hunt Cup he is generous and sound with his advice. He told me the story of what happened eight years before as if it were yesterday.

Part of the 118-year history of the Maryland Hunt Cup is its social side, and all of Maryland's hunting fraternity and past Hunt Cup luminaries turn out not only to witness the great spectacle but also to party – and how. The Maryland Hunt Cup is *the* social event of Maryland's annual timber-racing calendar. There is only the one race on the day, but for a number of days before and after it there are cocktail parties, lunches, Calcutta auctions where people bid for a ticket on each runner and the holder of the winning horse scoops the kitty, traditional post-race mint julep parties, and, for those lucky enough to be invited, there is a superb al-fresco race-day lunch given by course-owner Duck Martin and his wife Glennie at their home overlooking the track. Everywhere there is fantastic and friendly hospitality, bonhomie and banter.

The Cup is also, along with the Velká Pardubická in the Czech Republic, one of very few races that can genuinely vie with the Grand National at Aintree in terms of jumping ability, stamina and prestige. It is run over 4 miles and twenty-two separate upright timber fences. Numbers 6 and 16 stand over 5 feet high. Fence number 3 is the first real test, but none of them are small.

The second-last, with a small stream running under it, can catch out a few. This course is not for the faint-hearted, either horse or human. It is run in two loops but over different fences both times round. Two road crossings are well covered, and traffic, naturally, is stopped. Then, all traffic in the area would be heading for the Hunt Cup anyway.

Strictly for amateurs, the Hunt Cup, founded in 1894, is traditionally run on the fourth Saturday in April. It used to be for a trophy only, but nowadays a purse of $75,000 is shared out, with 60 per cent to the winner and the rest in reducing amounts down to sixth place. There is a photo finish, but there are no buildings or marquees of any sort. Jockeys change into their silks in a tent and weigh out on a scale carried onto the course and placed on a concrete well cap. Numerous small gazebos are scattered around spectators' cars, and sumptuous picnics are spread out. There are no hot-dog stalls, no merchandise and no grandstand: the steep hill overlooking the entire Worthington Valley gives a perfect view of the race as it unfolds.

It has changed little since the heady days of Jay Trump and Mountain Dew, who both won the race three times. Mountain Dew also finished runner-up to Jay Trump in each of his three wins.

Jay Trump's early career was chequered, to say the least. His dam's owner, Jay Sensenich from Pennsylvania, had chosen a particular sire in Maryland with the plan that the resulting progeny could run at the half-mile track at Charles Town, West Virginia. When the mare, Be Trump, came into season, she refused to load into the horsebox, leaving the owner in a dilemma. It happened that recuperating on his farm at that time was a stallion by the name of Tonga Prince, who had run in 'claimers' (the lowest rank of horse race) on the flat but had broken down (strained a tendon). Tonga Prince was the son of a champion sprinter called Polynesian, but his own racing ability appeared limited.

Although well enough bred herself by Australian champion Bernborough, Be Trump had poor conformation, a bad temperament and a worse race record – she only managed to win once in twenty-nine attempts.

The result of this unlikely mating was a good-sized bay colt with a large white star and a streak of white on his nose: Jay Trump, destined to win the world's greatest steeplechases and to enter the exclusive Hall of Fame. He was also blessed with a kind and willing temperament and was so well schooled by Tommy Smith that when he arrived at Fred Winter's embryo yard in Lambourn in 1964, prior to his crack at the 1965 Grand National, the 'boss' and his lads, Brian Delaney and Richard Pitman, found him a dream ride, almost like a dressage horse.

With his unexpected and distinctly moderate breeding, high things could scarcely have been expected of Jay Trump on the racecourse. Indeed, very little went right for him as a two-year-old in training. Avalyn Hunter tells the story of the accident that was to see Jay Trump scarred but unbowed for the rest of his life:

> While still an unraced two-year-old, he was struck in
> the head by his exercise boy for drifting out on a turn
> during a workout. The blow hit the colt in the eye and
> he ducked away, jumped the infield rail, and ran straight

into a post, laying his right foreleg open from elbow to knee. The injury healed well enough and never gave Jay Trump any soundness problems, but it left an unsightly scar that the horse carried to his dying day.[1]

Once on the track as a three-year-old, Jay Trump proved slow – too slow even to win a modest claiming race in eight attempts at the lowest grade. There must have been something about him – maybe his size, his scope, his equable temperament – that caught the eye of an amateur on the lookout for a 'timber' prospect for a friend of his mother's, Mary C. Stephenson (later LeBlond), herself a polo player and Joint Master of the Camargo Hunt. That amateur bought Jay Trump for $2,000.

Tommy Smith was born and bred to horses: his grandfather, Harry Worcester-Smith, once shipped his pack of hounds to Ireland for a season's hunting, and his father, Crompton, was a dairy farmer who also rode in local races. Tommy was first taken hunting in a basket saddle at the age of six months, and as a child he was inspired by a picture of the Grand National hanging over the fireplace. As soon as he could, he was riding anything and everything, and he gave up a place in college to pursue a career as an amateur rider.

One of the first things Tommy Smith did was to have Jay Trump gelded, and shortly after the horse was over that routine operation he started to teach him to jump. He also schooled him in flat work. This was in 1961–2, when, as part of his education, Tommy entered the then four-year-old into green hunter and

---

1   Avalyn Hunter, 'Jay Trump', Thoroughbred Horse Pedigrees, http://www.tbhorse-pedigree.com/library/horse/Jay%20Trump.htm (accessed 31 May 2012).

middleweight hunter classes locally, winning both and earning the Master's trophy and the title Grand Champion of the Trial. A season of regular hunting followed with the Green Spring Valley Hounds. The hunt Master, Bobby Fenwick, also hunted him on occasion and trained him up until after his first Maryland Hunt Cup. Tommy had already schooled the youngster well. The lovely-natured horse possessed innate good manners. The hunting taught him adaptability, quick-wittedness and a 'fifth leg' to extricate himself from tricky situations across country.

In his first timber race that spring, a girl jockey was put up. Jay Trump, surprisingly, after all his hunting, appeared at a loss. Thereafter, for the rest of his career, and even after a change of trainer (D. Michael Smithwick took over for his last two Cups), it was always Tommy who had the ride. Jay Trump won his remaining four point-to-points that season.

The following year, at just six years of age, Tommy felt Jay Trump was ready for America's supreme jumping test and entered him for the Maryland Hunt Cup. Also in the field was Mountain Dew, and the pair were destined to become long-lasting rivals. It was 1963; Mountain Dew had finished third in 1961 when himself a six-year-old and had won it the following year. Now, at eight, he was in his prime. The ground was hard, and only five horses ran. Two fell at the tenth. Jay Trump pulled hard, and Tommy Smith later recalled,

> He scared me that day, he was just plain getting too
> confident – too bold. He took off with me and I was
> strictly a passenger. And jump big! Sometimes he stood

back two or three strides. At the twelfth he stood so
far back that he landed on the top rail. It staggered
him, and scratched him up to his stifle. The rail didn't
break. He's awfully strong or he would have been
down for sure. After that he jumped more sanely, but
he was running too fast for his own safety.[2]

Not surprisingly, with Mountain Dew and Hurdy Gurdy both
pressing him, Jay Trump won in a new record time.

The following year he was fitted with a stronger Pelham bit,
and it was soon apparent that his second Hunt Cup was there for
the taking. So it proved, with him again beating Mountain Dew.
He had now won the My Lady's Manor Point-to-Point, the Grand
National Point-to-Point and the Maryland Hunt Cup. It was after
this that thoughts of the Aintree Grand National were first mooted.

The foray to England was executed with military precision.
Jay Trump arrived at Lambourn eight months before the Grand
National. (He had to run a number of times in England to qualify
and get handicapped.) Tommy followed four months later. From
the time of his arrival, he walked, talked, worked and practically
slept with the horse.

Jay Trump was the first equine incumbent, and then the first
runner, for brilliant jockey and horseman – and now brand-new
trainer – Fred Winter (my racing hero), whose application for a
job as a starter had been rejected. He won three of his five prep

---

2   Peter Winants, *Jay Trump, A Steeplechasing Saga*, with chapters contributed by W.
     Snowden Carter and Raymond G. Woolfe, Baltimore, Md.: Winants Bros., 1966.
     Quoted in John Ellis Rossell, Jr., *The Maryland Hunt Cup Past and Present*, Balti-
     more, Md.: The Sporting Press, p. 129.

races, but, as the big race loomed, all bar two of the horses in the yard went down with flu. When the other horse succumbed, Tommy Smith moved Jay Trump into isolation in a stable half a mile away. Even Fred Winter himself had to make an appointment to visit him and step through disinfectant at the entrance. Only one other horse throughout the various Lambourn stables escaped the illness – and that was another American visitor. Both had been vaccinated. (Flu vaccinations have long since been compulsory for racehorses in the UK.)

Saturday, 27 March 1965, was the first of the numerous 'last Grand Nationals' of a dozen years, the race threatened initially by owner Mrs Mirabel Topham's desire to sell the land for property development.

Jay Trump and Tommy Smith, both benefiting from concentrated tuition by Fred Winter, lined up close to the inside against forty-six rivals. It was a very different experience to any of Jay Trump's Maryland Hunt Cups where, with such high and solid timber fences, most years barely a dozen competed. Maybe it was this increased tension that caused him to kick out at the start, catching another runner, Leslie. Luckily the horse was unhurt and able to run.

Even without original top weight, the mighty Mill House, it was a good class field with such as the Queen Mother's The Rip, classy Rondetto and Scottish horse Freddie, the favourite, in the field. The absence of Mill House meant that most of the runners' weights were raised to 10 stone 13 pounds, making for a very cramped handicap in what is meant to be the greatest handicap race in the world. (The rules were changed following the emergence of Arkle in the same era, one handicap with the top weight declared to run, and an alternative handicap without.) Jay Trump was on 11 stone 5 pounds, along with The Rip and Mr Jones (third for another amateur, Chris Collins), Rondetto and Kapeno had 11 stone 6 pounds, and Freddie was top weight with 11 stone 10 pounds.

Tommy had learnt well from Fred Winter and had watched many films of past Nationals. He took the 'Brave Man's Route' down the inside (where the drop fences are bigger). Throughout the race Jay Trump could be seen just lobbing along, comfortably within himself. After Maryland, the fences were unlikely to be a problem.

The pair avoided a big pile-up at the first Becher's Brook – horses and riders scattered in every direction – and then, in a move that really saw his dressage training pay dividends, they cut such a fantastic tight angle at the Canal Turn that they saved many lengths. At the thirteenth fence they avoided disaster as a loose horse cut across the field, and from the end of the first circuit Jay Trump gradually moved up into contention. At the twenty-sixth, Rondetto fell in front of him. In avoiding him and his rider, Jay Trump showed the sort of agility that was later associated with Red Rum. Over the last two fences it was a two-horse race between Freddie and Jay Trump. On the run-in, Tommy picked up his whip. Jay Trump swished his tail in resentment and back-pedalled. To his credit, after a few strides of this, Tommy calmly put down his whip again, rode out with hands and heels . . . and the all-American partnership prevailed by three-quarters of a length. They had won the world's greatest steeplechase. It was a long way from running in the lowest class of flat races round the little-known circuits of the eastern USA.

Before returning to America, Jay Trump attempted the elusive Grande Course de Haies d'Auteuil (the French 'Grand National') and finished third after leading over the last fence. Fred Winter went on record to say that had Jay Trump remained in England he believed he was good enough to win a Cheltenham Gold Cup.

Back home he went, where it was announced that his final race would be the 1966 Maryland Hunt Cup. During the season that Jay Trump was away in England, Mountain Dew had won the Cup again. Going into 1966, the score between the pair was two apiece (though Mountain Dew had beaten Jay Trump in the 1963 and 1966 timber Grand National point-to-point, held the week before the Cup). Anticipation was high, and the cocktail parties were abuzz with debate on which horse would win.

The rain poured for a week before the race, leaving heavy ground. Once more, it was demonstrated that a really high-class horse can succeed on any ground. To the roar of the crowd in their perfect viewing vantage on the hill, the runners got under way. Jay Trump slipped on his approach to the 5-foot-high sixth fence, took off too close and clipped the top rail. He stayed on his feet, galloped on past the far woods, and by the time he reached the nineteenth fence he had a clear lead over Mountain Dew. He galloped home eight lengths clear – and into honourable retirement. For good measure, Mountain Dew himself won the race for a third time the following year, in 1967.

Jay Trump retired to Mrs Stephenson's Meshewa Farm, where he lived until 1988, cared for by her granddaughter Serena.

After his death, he was buried at the finish line of Kentucky Horse Park's steeplechase course.

Tommy Smith also bowed out at the top of his game and retired from race-riding. He trained for about a year and then left the horse world altogether. The lure remained in his blood, and, in time, Tommy came back to the horses only to suffer that dreadful fall, a cruel irony for the man who had conquered the amazing Maryland Hunt Cup three times as well as the Grand National at Aintree.

7

Nijinsky

Like a naughty little schoolboy full of high jinks and 'boldness', Nijinsky was a horse who needed his youthful exuberance to be channelled in the right direction from the start. In unsympathetic hands, he might have gone the wrong way. Luckily, the Canadian-bred colt found himself with perhaps the most outstanding trainer of all time: Vincent O'Brien.

O'Brien's genius we have glimpsed when he had Cottage Rake and was just embarking on his training career from a small farm in Churchtown, Co. Cork. He was mostly training jumpers but landed one or two mighty flat-racing gambles that put him on his feet. Apart from Cottage Rake's three Gold Cups and Hatton's

Grace's three Champion Hurdles, and another Gold Cup with Knock Hard, O'Brien also achieved the unprecedented feat of training the winner of the Grand National in three successive years from 1953 to 1955 with three different horses: Early Mist, Royal Tan and Quare Times. He also cleaned up at the Gloucestershire Hurdle (now the Supreme Novices) on numerous occasions, and in 1953 he won his first classic with Chamier in the Irish Derby.

This record would be beyond the dreams of most. And yet O'Brien was to top it. In 1951, he moved to a farm in Tipperary by the name of Ballydoyle, ripped out gaps in the hedgerows to allow for gallops and refurbished the house room by room (the horses and stables were probably done first). Bit by careful bit, he built up Ballydoyle into the world's best training centre.

Before the swinging sixties had got under way, O'Brien had transferred entirely to the flat. Apart from Chamier in the Irish Derby, he had already recorded an English classic win in the St Leger with Ballymoss (who also won the Irish Derby) and an Irish 2,000 Guineas with El Toro.

A chance remark by one of his owners, Jack Mulcahy, altered his life still further in 1971. Jack said, 'I can't understand you remaining only a trainer!' He suggested O'Brien should have a slice of the spoils; after all, due to his training, the horses were earning megabucks for their owners. It sowed the seed that was to grow into partnerships, syndicates, shares in racehorses and stallions and the setting up and expansion of Coolmore. The first man in to this new operation was Coolmore's then owner, Tim Vigors, and when he relinquished the reins Coolmore was headed by a triumvirate of Robert Sangster, John Magnier and Vincent O'Brien himself.

The trio wanted the best blood to build up their bloodstock empire and to stand their own stallions. To achieve that, they would have to go to America – but such a colt, with a proven track record and the promise of a bright stud career, would cost 'zillions'. They set about buying well-bred American yearlings, training them in Tipperary and, for those who 'made it' as racehorses, standing them at Coolmore Farm, just down the road from Ballydoyle. Within a quarter of a century Coolmore was to be as famous a stud as Ballydoyle was becoming as a training establishment: together, they made the perfect marriage.

In August 1968, O'Brien boarded a plane to Canada. It was a couple of months after his Epsom Derby success with the great Sir Ivor, and he was on a mission for Charles W. Englehard Jr., the American industrialist, who wanted O'Brien to look at a particular yearling for him. Englehard enjoyed life to the full, not only owning racehorses in many parts of the world but also taking part in big-game hunting, fishing, speed boating and poker playing. He died in his early fifties.

When he got to Canada, O'Brien preferred a different horse, by the then unknown sire, Northern Dancer. Englehard deferred to his preference, and O'Brien paid out a record sum, for Canada, at Woodbine Sales. The bright bay colt with black limbs, white heart-shaped star between his eyes and three white feet was to be named Nijinsky.

Back home in Ballydoyle, it soon became apparent that the fiery and temperamental colt was not going to be easy to train. In fact, he was so difficult to ride that O'Brien wrote to the owner expressing concern that the horse might never be moulded the right way. It was possible that the expensive purchase would never even reach the racetrack.

At first Nijinsky wouldn't eat the new food. Then he baulked at being led out of the stable, and, once out, he would rear and paw the air. Frequently he stubbornly refused to work, and invariably he would work himself up into a lather, sweating profusely. It was a wonder he had any flesh left on him.

It was thanks to his work riders – consummate horsemen with strength and patience, who never resorted to the 'cosh' – coupled with O'Brien's innate understanding of horses that Nijinsky became a little more tractable. He had to be ridden out first thing in the morning and worked alone. He still reared frequently, sweated profusely and, on occasion, did his best to dislodge his riders. Then the penny dropped, and Nijinsky came to hand – if not like a lamb then certainly like a lion roaring to go out and win.

And win is exactly what he did: eleven times in succession until twice beaten at the tail of his career. His ability on the racecourse was immediately apparent, and, interestingly, he sweated far less there. He won all five of his two-year-old races at odds-on. He won his first race, at the Curragh in July, so easily, that all of Ireland was abuzz. He followed up with three more Curragh victories that summer of 1969, so that by the time he first visited England racegoers were agog to see this new wonder horse.

They didn't have long to wait: the Dewhurst Stakes at Newmarket in September is a recognised classic trial for the cream of the two-year-old crop, and frequently its winner will become winter favourite for the following spring's 2,000 Guineas or the Derby. Nijinsky won so impressively that his record Canadian sales price now looked bargain basement. It is a testament to O'Brien's talent that he had succeeded in bringing the horse to the racecourse at all.

Nijinsky had settled so much that, as part of his winter break, O'Brien was able to turn him out in a paddock by day quite safely. During the winter he grew some more, furnished up and blossomed; his coat shone like burnished mahogany. Charles Englehard, O'Brien, jockeys Lester Piggott and, in Ireland, Liam Ward, work-riders Danny O'Sullivan and Johnny Brabston and his stable lad, to say nothing of the entire racing community on both sides of the Irish Sea, looked forward to his reappearance on the track at the start of the new decade.

Twenty years had passed since Cottage Rake's Cheltenham feats. Now here was a flat racehorse, only two years after Sir Ivor, who looked as if he might remain unbeaten. First up on the agenda was the 2,000 Guineas at Newmarket in May, a race founded in 1809 by Sir Charles Bunbury (who was to own the 1813 winner Smolensko). The 1,000 Guineas for fillies was inaugurated in 1814.

The Guineas is the first of the classics and is run over 1 mile at Newmarket in May. The Derby and Oaks follow at Epsom in June over a distance of 1½ miles, and the final leg of the 'Triple Crown' is the oldest classic, the St Leger, nowadays reduced to 1¾ miles at Doncaster in September. Nijinsky was a hot favourite for the 1970 2,000 Guineas and won like a 'good thing'.

Next stop, the Derby. Would the razzmatazz of the occasion flip that head of his? Before the race, there was an outbreak of coughing in Ballydoyle – just as there had been in Lambourn before Jay Trump's Grand National five years before. Like Tommy

Smith with that horse, O'Brien took no chances. He organised for Nijinsky to fly over early to England and to be stabled at and worked on Sandown Racecourse. The arrangement was a closely guarded secret: Nijinsky was hot property. O'Brien wanted him out of the way not only of flu germs but also of touts and, in particular, any would-be dopers. In the end, it was none of these that caused the scare that came very close to Nijinsky being unable to run in the 1970 Epsom Derby.

In those days the Derby was run on a Wednesday (since the mid-1990s it has been staged on a Saturday). The day after his arrival at Sandown, Nijinsky went out for a little trot around the place, loosening up his muscles after his journey. On the Sunday, he was given a half-speed workout. He worked faster the next day and was transported to Epsom. There, he did his final pre-Derby workout on part of the Derby course along with Ribofilio, working uphill for half a mile, walking down Tattenham Hill, and then just cantering back along the last few furlongs past what, in less than two days, would be the Derby winning post. The work went well – not a bother – and lovely Nijinsky returned to the stables.

Then he started pawing the ground – but not in his old, temperamental way; he was swinging his neck and head around towards his stomach, getting down to roll and getting straight up again, and walking restlessly around the straw-filled stable. He was showing the classic symptoms of colic. Just as with babies, this is a nasty, painful, gaseous complaint. But babies can get sick. Horses cannot. In severe cases, colic can lead to a twisted gut and almost certain death. It is one of the most distressing, drawn-out and excruciatingly painful complaints to witness; an operation might or might not save the animal. In mild to moderate cases, the normal remedy is to inject the horse with a muscle relaxant, and usually this is sufficient to enable the problem to pass. With just over a day before the race, this could not be a solution for Nijinsky because, quite rightly, of doping laws. Messages and vets were flying around between Epsom and Tipperary but basically nothing more than walking the horse round in circles could be done within the confines of Turf regulations. O'Brien watched on; for once he was helpless.

At last Nijinsky appeared less distressed. He looked more or less himself. And then he ate a little bran mash. By the evening he seemed right as rain. The actual attack had only lasted one and a half hours, a 'mild' bout, but it had seemed an eternity. Would it leave its mark?

There is nothing like Epsom on Derby Day. Much as in the nineteenth century, it remains a magnet out on the Downs for coach loads of trippers, for betting, beer tents, funfair booths and rides and Gypsies selling lucky heather. There are stalls for cockles and mussels, ice-cream vans, hot dogs and burgers, soothsayers, tipsters and crowds determined to enjoy their day out. All they have to look out for, apart from losing money on the horses, are the mingling pickpocketers.

There has been racing on Epsom Downs since, it is believed, 1625, following the discovery in 1618 of therapeutic water containing a type of salt that is used as a purgative (still known as Epsom salts). The little village of Epsom became a fashionable spa, and the visiting gentry liked to while away their time with a bit of horse racing on the nearby horseshoe-shaped chalk downs. Epsom's gradients, and the famous Tattenham Corner, around which many an ungainly colt has become unbalanced and lost his place, are the ultimate test for Thoroughbreds, many of whom spend their racing days on flat, featureless tracks and so, although no longer the world's richest race, the Derby remains one of the most highly regarded.

By ancient rights the Downs are common land, but an Act of Parliament in 1936 closed the racecourse itself, the grandstands complex and the training gallops to the general public. On Derby Day, within the enclosures on the other side of the course from the open downs, morning-suited and top-hatted men vie with well-dressed women to catch a glimpse of the horses in the parade ring, from the grandstands or along the rails. The wide grass course is manicured to perfection, and the atmosphere is fraught with anticipation. Even the calmest of horses sometimes 'flip'. For them, there is not the usual canter to the start as they leave the paddock. Instead, they have to mill around getting into alphabetical order and then parading in front of the stands. For three-year-old Thoroughbred colts (and just occasionally a filly), the buzz, the noise and the crowds can be too much, and some will boil over, losing their race before it has even started.

Derby Day dawned, and although Nijinsky was favourite, he started at odds against, for what would be the only time in his career. Not a whisper of the colic scare had come out, but there was a particular French horse in the field, Gyr, who was so highly thought of that his trainer, Etienne Pollet, had postponed his retirement for a year.

Nijinsky got through the lengthy preliminaries undaunted, and Lester Piggott, backside poised in his own inimitable fashion, settled him nicely in the race. The runners negotiated Tattenham Corner and swept down the hill and into the home straight, where, with 2 furlongs to go, Gyr set sail for home. From the stands it must have looked as if Etienne Pollet had been right.

Then Lester Piggott simply shook up the reins on Nijinsky, and the beautiful colt smoothly changed up into overdrive. He swooped past his rival with his ears pricked to score easily by two and a half lengths in a new record time. It was a truly brilliant performance, franked by Gyr's subsequent easy win in the Grand Prix de St Cloud. For many racing aficionados, the memory of this victory shines as brightly today as it did on Derby Day forty years ago.

After the Derby there was inevitably talk of the Triple Crown, last won thirty-five years before in 1935 by Bahram. Even by 1970 the Prix de l'Arc de Triomphe had usurped the St Leger in prestige, and this was the colt's long-term goal. Before that, there was both the Irish Derby and then the King George VI and Queen Elizabeth Stakes at Royal Ascot, traditionally the first time three-year-olds take on older horses at 1½ miles.

A few weeks after the Derby win, on firm ground, Nijinsky appeared before his adoring home crowd in heavy rain for the Irish Derby – and easily romped to his ninth successive win. While the race proved easy, in the preliminaries Nijinsky sweated up, much as he used to as a youngster at home. Until that day, he had shown no signs of it on the racecourse. Nothing, not even the wet, could dampen his performance.

Royal Ascot comes quite quickly after the English and Irish Derbies, but Nijinsky took it in his stride. He was the only three-year-old and lined up against impressive opposition, including the previous year's Derby winner, Blakeney, but yet again he toyed with the rest of the field, drawing away from Blakeney with ease.

He was being hailed as Horse of the Century and returned home to a rapturous welcome. And then he contracted ringworm – the wretched condition covered him. Debilitating at any time, suddenly the tilt at the Triple Crown seemed in danger. Nevertheless, Nijinsky came right in time and duly won the St Leger and the Triple Crown – but at a cost.

The St Leger is the oldest classic and was founded in 1776, allowing younger horses (three-year-olds) to race over what was then the short distance of 2 miles, compared with the more usual 4 miles. When, in 1853, a horse called West Australian achieved the feat of winning all three classics for the first time, the phrase 'Triple Crown' was coined. Since then, just fourteen horses have won it, and only one jockey has won it twice: Steve Donoghue, with Pommern (1915) and Gay Crusader (1917). Always popular with the public and his peers, Steve never once got into trouble with the stewards. He retired in 1937 having been Champion Jockey ten times and having won six Derbies.

These days, for commercial stud reasons, the Triple Crown is seldom attempted. Breeders want speed over stamina, and to win the St Leger will, rightly or wrongly, reduce the value of a sire. Nijinsky was the last winner in 1970, and since then only Nashwan (1989) and Sea The Stars (2009) would have been eligible to try, being the only two to have won the first two legs of the Guineas and the Derby. Horse breeding has become more distance-related, and a 'Guineas' horse is generally considered unlikely to stay the Derby distance, while a Derby winner will seldom have the greater speed needed to win the Guineas. In recent times, only Irish trainer Jim Bolger has publicly stated that he would attempt the Triple Crown, with Teofilo, who had been an exceptional two-year-old, but a matter of days before the first leg, the 2007 Guineas, he met with a setback and was withdrawn.

Frankel, in 2011, won the 2,000 Guineas by a record-breaking ten lengths but was not even entered for the Derby. Sea The Stars is a half-brother to Galileo, being out of the same Arc-winning dam, but while Galileo, by Sadler's Wells, was fully expected to get the Derby distance, there was considerable humming and hawing over whether Sea The Stars, being by the miler Cape Cross, would run in it. Equally, Galileo did not run in the 2,000 Guineas but won the Derby Trial in Leopardstown instead. It takes an exceptional horse to win the first two legs of the Triple Crown, never mind all three.

The St Leger would surely have been his for the taking had Sea The Stars been entered, and, as a 2,000 Guineas winner he had proved he had the speed required of a top stallion. Even so, his 2009 win in the Prix de l'Arc de Triomphe was one of horse racing's epic moments and will live for ever in the memory of those lucky enough to have witnessed it.

It would be the view of many a pundit that human error rather than ringworm caused the defeat of lovely Nijinsky in the 'Arc'. Perhaps it was a combination of both. Lester Piggott was so confident of his mount that he lay far, far out of his ground. He came with Nijinsky's fabulous turn of foot and may have momentarily headed the outsider Sassafras, but he didn't carry the advantage through. Nijinsky's unbeaten record was lost by a head.

One of thousands of spectators that day was a young seminarian, Vincent (Vince) Murray, and his friend, Jim Carroll, now Parish Priest in Carlingford; they were taking in the Arc on their way to Rome. In his pocket, Vincent (now a lay teacher of theology and happily married with a family) had his money for the term ahead. He put half of it on Nijinsky to win, thinking he would be making easy money. He recalls, 'Nijinsky was coming through to win. And he didn't. I just sat there, head down, and a lady turned to me and asked if I was really that disappointed. I didn't answer, but I have never, since that day, backed an odds-on favourite.'

Instead of retiring Nijinsky to stud after the Arc, it was decided to let him have one more 'easy' win, in the Champion Stakes. This time he reverted to his juvenile antics of rearing, sweating and acting distraught. He was beaten soundly into second place. At stud, Nijinsky produced no fewer than three Epsom Derby winning sons – Golden Fleece in 1982, Shahrastani in 1986 (in which year he also sired Kentucky Derby winner, Ferdinand) and the unbeaten chestnut Lammtarra in 1995 – and two Epsom Derby winning grandsons: Kahyasi in 1988 and the flaxen Generous in 1991.

8

Golden Cygnet

Gone but not forgotten. The number of people who suggested Golden Cygnet as a 'must-have' for this book is remarkable bearing in mind the brevity of his career and how long ago it was – more than thirty years. The impression he left on the racing world in that short time so long ago is indelible. No sport is ever without its 'what might have been' stories, but there are aficionados today who can still barely mention brilliant 2011 champion hurdler Hurricane Fly, winner of eleven Grade 1 hurdles, in the same breath.

What made the bay so special in his short life? For most, it was the way he came up the famous – infamous – Cheltenham hill to the finishing line in the 1978 Supreme Novices Hurdle – the accepted route for promising youngsters to take on their way to the following year's Champion Hurdle. The incline that has been the undoing of so many seemingly top horses saw Golden Cygnet simply pulling further and further ahead from his rivals to storm away with the Festival prize – and straight into ante-post favouritism for the following year's Champion Hurdle. Never before or since has the style with which he won been emulated, let alone surpassed.

Golden Cygnet was by the horse who was to become one of the all-time great National Hunt sires, Deep Run. Dawn Run is his best-known progeny, but Golden Cygnet was from his first crop, therefore completely unproved, and stood at a modest fee. What's more, neither his dam nor grand-dam ever raced, and Golden Cygnet was also an only foal, so on breeding alone high things would not have been expected of him.

Bred by Mr J. T. O'Brien, the choice of Deep Run would have been relatively simple: he was cheap, and he was local. He stood at Sandville Stud, Glanworth, near Fermoy in Co. Cork, which, along with Beeches Stud, Tallow, was one of the two National Hunt branches of Coolmore Stud in Co. Tipperary. It was traditional throughout Ireland, and in Co. Cork in particular, for farmers to keep one or two Thoroughbred mares and so the stud location was convenient for many National Hunt breeders.

Deep Run himself was not a striking stallion, and his colour, chestnut, was against him for breeders' choice. Neither was his race record outstanding, but it was good enough to become one of the all-time-great National Hunt sires. He was by Pampered King out of a mare by Court Martial, and he won four races, two of them at Grade 2, which saw him head the Irish two-year-olds list in 1968, the year that Sir Ivor won the Derby. He was also second in that year's Dewhurst Stakes to Ribofilio – Charles Englehard's colt who was to be used as work companion for Nijinsky at Epsom prior to the 1970 Derby. At three, Deep Run was second in the Irish St Leger to Reindeer, and at four he finished second to Nijinsky, no less, in the Gladness Stakes.

Deep Run had run well in the highest class, but, nevertheless, had only scored as a two-year-old. Rising five, he was despatched to the Newmarket December Sales, where horses off the flat are often bought to go hurdling. On his jumping debut, Deep Run won a 2-mile novice hurdle at Doncaster ridden by Terry Biddlecombe. He ran twice more, and, having not been gelded, he retired to stud in 1971.

By the very nature of the jumping game, a stallion is often in his senior years before his progeny 'make it' for him. By contrast, a colt that retires from the flat at three can be producing winners three years later and classic winners only a year after that.

Before he had made it as a successful sire, Deep Run was to produce Golden Cygnet, foaled in 1972, from his first crop. He became a perennial leader of the National Hunt Sires list in the 1980s and 1990s, and while Dawn Run, National Hunt's greatest ever mare, is his best known, he also produced Ekbalco, Daring Run and Fifty Dollars More as well as Another Breeze, Half Free, Deep Gale, Kas and full brothers Morley Street and Granville Again, who both won the Champion Hurdle (1991 and 1993).

All of these names were in the future when Golden Cygnet was consigned to the Goffs November Sales of 1975, and this was reflected in his price. The three-year-old was picked up for 980 guineas by Edward O'Grady, then a trainer in his twenties, and his new owner became Raymond Rooney.

Rooney was a highly regarded person in many aspects of life and, in later years, was appointed a member of the Turf Club and the Irish National Hunt Steeplechase Committee, a senior steward, a trustee of the Turf Club and a vice-chairman of the Club's appeals body. His heart lay in Galway, where he established his business, Rooney Auctioneers and Chartered Surveyors, in the 1960s, and where he was Chairman not only of the Galway Race Committee but also Fáilte Ireland West – he was influential in the successful Volvo Ocean Race festival shortly before his death. He was the Chairman of Croí, the West of Ireland Cardiology Foundation and, for good measure, Honorary Norwegian Consul in Ireland. He was also well known as an accomplished tennis player and lifelong member of the Galway Lawn and Tennis Club. He died 'in harness' in his Galway office in the summer of 2009.

In 1976, when Golden Cygnet's career began on the flat as a four-year-old, most of this was in the future for young Ray Rooney. The first race chosen for Golden Cygnet was a 2-mile flat maiden at Leopardstown on the June Bank Holiday. Clearly the money was down, for his price tumbled from 7–1 to 3–1. He won it all right, but then lost it in the stewards' room for causing interference.

His next run was in a bumper at Roscommon where he was a fast-finishing third, beaten less than a length, before gaining his first official win, by eight lengths, at Naas in a 1½-mile flat maiden for amateur riders in early October.

It was almost a year before Golden Cygnet reappeared in

public, finishing last in a handicap over 2 miles at Listowel in September before heading to Punchestown the following month for another handicap over a trip that was patently too short for him (9 furlongs). The form book stated 'never placed to challenge, some late progress'.

Readers of the form book who spotted that Golden Cygnet was entered for Leopardstown's November Handicap might have deduced that this was what he was perhaps being 'laid out' for, in the hope that he would be given a low weight in the last big handicap of the flat season. What was more, a top lightweight jockey from Britain had been booked, Richard Fox, who could do the light 7 stone 7 pounds weight allotted. Fox was known as the 'handicap king', and on the day Golden Cygnet was duly backed in from 20–1 down to 7–2.

He failed to settle in the early stages of the race and found himself in front with half a mile to run before fading in the straight to finish seventh behind the 2–1 favourite Mr Kildare, winning for the second successive year for the trainer–jockey combination of Liam Browne and Tommy Carmody.

The very next month, the life and career of Golden Cygnet were to alter dramatically when a switch to hurdling brought out his true talent, and he remained unbeaten thereafter until his final start. Niall 'Boots' Madden had already piloted Golden Cygnet to his only flat race win and was involved in the yard as its amateur. He had been schooling Golden Cygnet over hurdles at home and knew him well.

Golden Cygnet won in workmanlike fashion in a Clonmel maiden hurdle in December – in a copybook favourite's display of 'in touch, second three out, led between the last two, drew away to win by three lengths'. It was his performance on his next appearance in Leopardstown, on St Stephen's Day, that set people talking.

A part of the feature four-day Christmas Festival, this was a higher-class and much more valuable race, open only to previous winners – but yet again he started favourite. If 'the word was out' locally about him before this race it was about to go national. His manner of racing was to become his trademark: switching off early, but, like a rare hunter at the end of a long day's sport, instead of tiring he grew stronger and stronger towards the finish.

There were twelve runners in the Leopardstown race. Niall Madden held Golden Cygnet up early on in the race and gradually made progress to join the leaders approaching the straight. Seeing daylight ahead of him, all Golden Cygnet wanted to do was gallop on. Naturally, his jockey wanted to restrain him, to 'save something for the finish', but Golden Cygnet would have none of it, and Madden found them leading earlier than intended. It made no difference: Golden Cygnet simply cantered away from the opposition to win on a tight rein by a massive twenty lengths.

Less than two weeks later, and fighting fit at home, Golden Cygnet ran in the Slaney Hurdle at Naas. He won, as expected, but not without a battle. Again there was a stewards' enquiry into possible interference, but this time he deservedly kept the race.

He was given a break and next appeared at the late February meeting at Punchestown, a prep for Cheltenham and also home of a Grand National trial. He faced six opponents, but they may as well have been running solely for place money, for the race brought the star back to his dream role of winning impressively on a tight rein. It was all systems go for Cheltenham and the young Golden Cygnet.

Wednesday, 15 March 1978, saw perfect ground for the middle day of the Festival. All eyes would be on the feature Waterford Crystal Champion Hurdle later in the afternoon, but to open proceedings was the tantalising prospect of 'the good thing' coming over from Ireland for the Waterford Crystal Supreme Novices Hurdle. Pitched against the seventeen best novice hurdlers that England and Ireland could muster, Golden Cygnet would have his biggest task to date on hand. Or would he?

Amateur Niall Madden retained the ride, as usual, no matter that he was against the best professionals. He knew the horse like no other. Madden kept Golden Cygnet covered up in the early stages as first Leirum and then Prousto (ridden by Jonjo O'Neill) led the pack. Golden Cygnet was quite content to lob along, without fighting for his head, as normal 'pullers' might do, but once Madden showed him daylight at the top of the hill on the final circuit, that was it. Golden Cygnet now pulled for his head and did his best to storm down the descent. Once on the level ground and round the last bend, approaching the second-last flight, Madden let out his reins a notch, and Golden Cygnet was gone. His speed was electrifying. He jumped the last two flights as well as he had the previous six: slick, smooth and fast. It was when the other horses were tiring, at the end of the race, that Golden Cygnet, by contrast, stepped up a gear, scorching up the hill in a devastating turn of foot and swiftly putting an astonishing fifteen lengths between himself and his nearest pursuer, Western Rose.

When Monksfield and veteran rider Tommy Kinane clinched a memorable Champion Hurdle an hour later, their winning time was a full second slower than that of Golden Cygnet. Truly, the hurdling world lay at his feet, and he was immediately installed ante-post favourite for the following year's Champion Hurdle.

He turned out for the Fingal Hurdle, contested by Ireland's best novice hurdlers, at the Fairyhouse Easter Festival, which features the Irish Grand National (won that year by the Jim Dreaper-trained Brown Lad). With Golden Cygnet at long odds-on, it was the now familiar pattern: tucked in, moved up at the business end of the race and then galloped clear in scintillating style to win by ten lengths.

It was to have been his last race of the season, with a well-earned summer break ahead, but when he returned to Edward O'Grady's stables at Ballynonty, Co. Tipperary, he was so full of himself that connections decided to let him run in the Scottish Champion Hurdle at Ayr. Although it would be a step up in class to take on existing and former Champion Hurdlers, his form had been so consistent, and, at six years of age, he was not too raw and young.

Punters and bookmakers complimented him by sending him off joint favourite with future dual Champion Hurdler Sea Pigeon (1980, 1981). Night Nurse, winner the previous two years (1976 and 1977) and the useful Beacon Light were also in the line-up. As the race unfolded, it looked, again, a case of déjà-vu: held up, smooth move forward, poised behind leader Night Nurse and slightly ahead of Sea Pigeon at the last on his usual tight rein, ready to explode up the run-in . . . but he took off a fraction too early, clipped the top of the hurdle and crashed to the ground on his neck. Madden was thrown clear. Sea Pigeon had been slightly hampered by the fall but just held off Night Nurse.

After a number of minutes, Golden Cygnet got to his feet – to a crescendo of cheers from the anxious spectators in the stands. He was a little wobbly perhaps, but he was alive, and able to walk back to the racecourse stables.

There, with a lump swelling on his neck, it was agreed to take him to the Royal Veterinary College in Edinburgh as a precaution. For two days the reports were upbeat. On the Monday night, after returning late to his Tipperary home from an evening meeting at Kilbeggan, O'Grady at last relaxed, believing the danger to his star to be over, when the phone rang. When he heard the Scottish vet, he hoped it meant the horse was now ready to return home. Instead, he was told that Golden Cygnet, potentially the greatest hurdler of all time, had suffered a brain haemorrhage as a result of an injured vertebra and had been put down. That shattering call remains as fresh today for Edward O'Grady as it was in 1978.

He sums it up poignantly: 'For two days we'd entertained false hopes. It was devastating. Absolutely devastating. Rather like a friend or part of the family not only dying unexpectedly, but in a different country. That was the hardest part.'

The 1977/8 Timeform Annual stated:

> The race confirmed two important points – that Sea Pigeon had no superior among the established hurdlers apart from Monksfield, and that all the superlatives heaped on Golden Cygnet had been justified [. . .] Golden Cygnet appeared to have plenty left, and was two lengths up on Sea Pigeon and about to take the lead from Night Nurse when he suffered his fatal

fall. Judging by the way Golden Cygnet finished in his previous races, he would have taken some catching [. . .] The connections of Sea Pigeon did not dispute the general feeling afterward that Golden Cygnet would have beaten Sea Pigeon in the Scottish Champion Hurdle if he had not come to grief at the last. And for a novice to have defeated a seasoned campaigner of Sea Pigeon's calibre at a difference of only 1 lb would have been a staggering achievement.

More than thirty years on, and the racing world in general still believes Golden Cygnet was the best novice hurdler ever seen.

9

Istabraq

The loss of any horse is devastating for its connections, and when it is a horse of Golden Cygnet's young promise it is felt throughout the racing world. But the death of a young trainer is truly tragic, as it was in the case of John Durkan, the man who found and had faith in failed flat racer Istabraq.

John Durkan was the son of a builder and permit racehorse trainer and was fourteen when his father Bill famously trained Anaglog's Daughter. She won nineteen races in all, three on the flat, eleven hurdles and five chases, including at Cheltenham and Ascot, and she was also second in the Queen Mother Champion Chase and the King George VI Chase.

Ferdy Murphy, now a top trainer in Yorkshire, was Bill Durkan's hands-on assistant at the time.

The young John was hooked. He spurned joining his father's building business and headed to Lambourn, first to trainer Charlie Brooks, then to Oliver Sherwood as assistant trainer and finally to John Gosden. He became an accomplished amateur rider – and he lived life to the full, sharing a cottage with three other young racing men who became firm friends: Jamie Osborne, Eddie Hales and Ed Dunlop. Among his near century of winners he was victorious for both the Queen and the Queen Mother. He met and fell in love with Carol Hyde, a daughter of Tim and Patricia Hyde of Camas Park Stud, Cashel, Co. Tipperary, and soon after they married he set about becoming a trainer. His father, having failed to persuade him into the building business, not surprisingly would have liked him to take over his stables at Stepaside, beneath the Wicklow Mountains and a stone's throw from Leopardstown. John had made his contacts and his life in England, so Bill agreed to buy the Newmarket stable of Tom Jones, who was shortly to retire, which would give John security during what were sure to be the hard early years of getting himself established.

John sought out prospective owners, and, once he had enough (even allowing for a number who failed to follow through their verbal promises), the stage was set. All he wanted was one particular horse that he had known at John Gosden's – and an owner for him.

Sometimes there is no clue from either birth or breeding that a future star has been born. With Istabraq this was not the case. The surprise wasn't that he became famous, but rather what he became famous for. Istabraq was originally owned by Hamdan Al

Maktoum, who purchased his dam, Betty's Secret, after the death of her breeder, E. P. 'Eddie' Taylor. Taylor was the Canadian who had owned Nijinsky and who also stood Northern Dancer at his famed Windfields Farm. Betty's Secret was a half sister to a French Derby winner, and she herself bred Epsom Derby winner Secreto (by Secretariat).

Istabraq was by the great Sadler's Wells (by Northern Dancer), and, out of such a high-class mare, it was safe to assume he should be a classic prospect. No one could have foreseen that Istabraq (meaning either 'silk', 'brocade' or 'lightning' in Arabic; it is also a girl's name) would become one of the greatest hurdlers of all time.

He was helped into this world by Mullingar man Cyril O'Hara who at the time was managing the Maktoums' Derrinstown Stud in Co. Kildare, where the young Istabraq spent his formative first year of life. Although many foals were born there each season, Cyril remembers the birth of Istabraq in 1992. 'He was by Sadler's Wells who was all the rage, but Betty's Secret was the last mare on the stud that year to foal, so we had to wait until late May to see what she would produce.'

Betty's Secret was a mare who liked to be alone and, unusually for a brood mare, spurned the company of her fellow mares. Her labour was arduous, but at last a large, perfectly formed bay colt emerged. He had a big white star, three white socks and was the colour and stamp of his father.

When he was ready for breaking and to start his two-year-old flat-racing career, Istabraq was sent to John Gosden, who had been head-hunted from America back to Newmarket by the Maktoums to become one of their trainers. All too soon Gosden discovered his prospects of stardom with the colt were slight. It wasn't that Istabraq's 'wedding vegetables' caused problems (which would make him more interested in the fillies than in racing), but for a classic-bred horse he just wasn't fast enough.

He had foot problems, and then he chipped a fragment of bone in his knee. He was also slow maturing, and, as he progressed, some further pointers emerged: he stayed on at the end of his races; he was best when allowed to bowl along in front; he was tenacious in a battle – and he could be highly strung, often sweating profusely in pre-race preliminaries.

Istabraq finished down the field on his only run as a two-year-old and in his first two runs at three, before collecting a second place followed by his first win at Salisbury, where he pulled hard for Willie Carson, another second (at York) and then his second (and final) win on the flat up at Ayr. He was then favourite but finished down the field at Ascot that September of his third season racing, was second at Newbury and unplaced at Doncaster in November.

He was given one more chance at four, at Haydock Park in June, but in finishing second 'time' was called on his flat-racing career. Istabraq was despatched to the Tattersalls July Sales, where horses 'chucked out' by their flat-racing connections are often bought by National Hunt trainers as potential hurdlers.

John Durkan, meanwhile, had been working hard to find a prospective purchaser who would allow him to train the horse. The result of his efforts was that none other than J. P. McManus agreed to go up to 100,000 guineas for Istabraq. A nervous Durkan was afraid the horse would make more than that – but when the hammer came down at just 38,000 guineas, the first part of his training dream had come true. Durkan told J.P. that his new purchase would win the following spring's Royal Sun Alliance Novices Hurdle over 2 miles 5 furlongs at the Cheltenham National Hunt Festival. Even right back then, as a four-, coming five-year-old, it was staying races that were being considered Istabraq's likely forte. Durkan's prophecy was made with conviction: from the start he believed in his new charge, the horse that, he dreamed, might kick-start his embryonic training business.

Istabraq was despatched to the Hydes' home in Tipperary to be gelded, to recuperate, and then to come back to the Newmarket stables once he and they were ready. Meanwhile, Durkan continued attending sales to fill his initial order book. At one in Newmarket, he caught a 'cold'. He ignored it and travelled over to more sales in Ireland. The 'cold' turned into a rotten dose of 'flu' and then into 'pneumonia'. It was none of these. Durkan, aged thirty, had contracted leukaemia.

As a temporary measure, it was agreed that Aidan O'Brien would train Istabraq, just until Durkan recovered. No matter how successful Aidan was, and is, it was understood 100 per cent that Istabraq was 'John's horse'. A quality that Aidan O'Brien and J. P. McManus share is loyalty.

Durkan's harrowing and drawn-out illness, his brave battle and his determination to recover and train Istabraq, are well chronicled in Michael Clower's *The Legend of Istabraq*.[1] No one, least of all John Durkan, his wife or family, deserved the suffering. His father Bill sought out the best centre he could find; it was in New York, and it was from his hospital bed, usually with at least

---

1   Michael Clower, *The Legend of Istabraq*, London: Cassell, 2000.

one family member, that Durkan listened to Istabraq's initial hurdle races via mobile phone.

From the start, John Durkan, no matter how ill he was, could see 'his' horse fulfilling his dreams. In his first outing over hurdles, at a 2-mile novice event at Punchestown in November 1996, a jumping error at the final flight probably cost him the race, going down by only a head to the odds-on favourite, Noble Thyne. It was the only time John heard him beaten.

Just as Niall 'Boots' Madden rode Golden Cygnet in all seven of his hurdle races, another truly great relationship was forged with Istabraq. Charlie Swan rode him in all twenty-nine of his hurdle races – in fact, he postponed relinquishing his riding licence to see out the great star's career before concentrating on training.

For his second hurdle race, Istabraq romped away with the Royal Bond Novice Hurdle at Fairyhouse in December. Despite a mistake at the last he beat Palette by an easy four and a half lengths with Noble Thyne this time a long way back in third. It was then on to Leopardstown on 27 December – and John Durkan was flying home for Christmas. While Istabraq's facile win (beating Palette again) was probably John's best possible Christmas present, the greatest gift for his wife and family was undoubtedly seeing his happy smile in the winner's enclosure.

En route to the Cheltenham Festival, Istabraq would have one more race, while Durkan returned to New York for a bone-marrow transplant. Istabraq duly won his 'prep' race, again at Leopardstown – but only just. He made a number of mistakes and was headed by Finnegan's Hollow, also owned by J.P., on the run to the line. The tenacious, battling spirit that Istabraq had in common with his would-be trainer saw him prevail by a head.

John's transplant, meanwhile, was scheduled for 13 March 1997 – Gold Cup day at Cheltenham and, importantly to the patient, the day after 'his' horse was to contest the race he had originally staked him to win: the Royal Sun Alliance Novices Hurdle.

Istabraq was now officially five years old and was not only working well over a distance but was also showing such speed that the shorter Supreme Novices Hurdle (the more usual stepping stone to the Champion Hurdle) was considered. The original plan was adhered to, and in Durkan's New York hospital room, he and his wife Carol tuned in to the commentary relayed to them over a mobile phone. It was just as well that they could not see the preliminaries for, with the huge crowd and tense atmosphere that pervades Cheltenham during the Festival, Istabraq had become awash with sweat – much as Nijinsky had before the Arc.

Charlie Swan and his unsettled mount left the paddock early and cantered alone down to the start in an attempt to soothe the horse. That worked until the other sixteen horses arrived, and Istabraq, now white with lather, attempted to charge the starting tapes. For the restart, instead of jumping him off handily, Charlie Swan, thinking 'on his feet', changed plan and dropped him out last of all at the start. It worked. The horse began to relax.

In New York, John and Carol didn't hear his name called by the commentator at all – until they heard he was last. Last! Surely the jockey knew from his flat form that he had to be ridden from the front? Ill, exasperated and helpless, John Durkan was still able to swear. And he mustered enough strength to throw the phone down.

'He can't win from there,' he told his wife. Carol picked up the phone, listened for a moment and handed it back to John. Istabraq remained at the rear, nicely 'switched off' until they reached the top of the hill for the final time. From there, he gradually made up ground, responding to his rider's urgings.

As they approached the second-last flight, three horses were still ahead of them. Charlie Swan prayed for a gap to open up. Just in time it did. As he was taking off, another horse veered into him, causing them to collide in mid-air. There was a gasp from the crowd as it seemed Istabraq had to fall. Somehow he stayed upright, with Charlie Swan stuck like glue in the saddle. The stuffing had been knocked out of the horse. Charlie gave him time to regain his equilibrium, then they made up ground and actually managed to hold a slight lead at the last flight, closely attended by farmer's son, amateur Fred Hutsby on Mighty Moss.

Showing the courage that was to become his hallmark on the occasions he found himself in a fight, Istabraq would not give in. His rival was every bit as determined. The two horses fought every inch of the way up that famous finishing hill.

Istabraq held on.

John Durkan's long-held belief in him had been vindicated. The next day, courtesy of one of his four brothers (two had volunteered to be a donor), he received the bone-marrow transplant that was hoped would save his life.

Istabraq had a good break before reappearing in the 2½-mile Novice Champion Hurdle at Punchestown, Ireland's National Hunt Festival, at the end of April. Although he made a couple of now-customary mistakes, he won as he liked. In New York, Durkan was pleased to hear 'his' horse win again, but he was secretly disappointed at his own lack of progress since the transplant. It was discovered that the cancer had spread to his lymph glands, and then, all too soon afterwards, following a blackout, a brain scan revealed a cancerous spot. It was a dark, dark time.

Istabraq's easy opening win of the new 1997–8 season at Tipperary in October made John determined to be in Ireland for the next race, the Hatton's Grace Hurdle at Fairyhouse at the end of November. The Champion Hurdle the following March was now the declared aim.

The medics did not want him to move. At length, and much against their advice, they allowed him to fly to Ireland. Some things are meant to be. After meeting many friends and smiling happily in the winner's enclosure at Fairyhouse (an all-the-way win for Istabraq), followed by a visit to the shrine at Knock with his father, a further collapse ruled out John's booked return to New York. He was in a coma for several hours and was not expected to pull through, but suddenly he opened his eyes, sat up and made such an astonishing recovery that he was able to spend Christmas with his family. He missed Leopardstown, where Istabraq, at odds of 6–1 on, landed a facile victory in the 2-mile December Festival Hurdle.

Durkan was too ill to return to the hospital in New York. On 21 January, in his beloved home country of Ireland and with his whole family around him, John Durkan died. He was thirty-one years old. His funeral was held the day before Istabraq's next race, the AIG Europe Champion Hurdle at Leopardstown, which he duly won. J. P. McManus asked Carol Durkan to accept the trophy.

Less than eight weeks later, Istabraq won the first of his three Smurfit Champion Hurdles. That made ten wins in a row – and he did it very easily, by an outstanding twelve lengths, in spite of meeting seventeen accomplished opponents. He returned to rapturous applause with, seemingly, the whole racing world of Ireland and the UK cheering him. J. P. McManus told the waiting press reporters afterwards, 'I would never have been fortunate enough to own Istabraq but for John. Thinking about him makes us realise how lucky we are to be coming to Cheltenham. Winning is a bonus.'

Apart from the many tributes to John Durkan and his family, and the jockey Charlie Swan, there was a hail of praise on the horse himself. For sheer originality, my favourite is the one from Ladbrokes printed in *The Sporting Life*: 'Roofer required. Apply Cheltenham Racecourse.'

In his next race, the Martell Aintree Hurdle, Istabraq was beaten by a head, against an inspired A. P. McCoy ride on the Martin Pipe-trained Pridwell. It was then out to grass for his summer break at J.P.'s home in Co. Tipperary, before returning to his winning ways for the 1998–9 season, this time beginning in Cork (7–2 on), the Hatton's Grace again (5–1 on) and the Leopardstown Christmas meeting's Agri-Business December Festival Hurdle (10–1 on). At the AIG Europe Champion Hurdle in late January, Istabraq was taken on by the highly promising Ferdy Murphy-trained French Holly, but he dismissed this Champion Hurdle pretender easily and retained the title.

He was to do so again in the Smurfit Champion Hurdle, the ultimate hurdling crown, in March 1999. There were fourteen runners, but only Istabraq and French Holly in the betting. The bookmakers forgot to take into account, however, Theatreworld, who notched up an incredible third consecutive runner's-up berth in the Champion Hurdle, dividing Istabraq and French Holly.

It was now two Champion Hurdles for Istabraq – how many more were to come? The season was not yet over. Istabraq scored again easily for rider Charlie Swan, owner J. P. McManus and trainer Aidan O'Brien at both Aintree (the Martell) and Punchestown (Shell Champion), where his Irish home crowd cheered him to the hilt.

Istabraq's new season for 1999–2000 brought him back to his traditional Tipperary start, en route for a crack at a third Smurfit Champion Hurdle. Tipperary brought an easy win with a horse called Limestone Lad in second place, building a reputation for himself by making all to win staying races. A month later, when Istabraq was bidding for his third Hatton's Grace at a price of 7–1 on, Limestone Lad and Shane McGovern set up such a long lead that when Charlie Swan pressed the button Istabraq simply couldn't reach them.

For his customary Leopardstown Christmas date, Istabraq was back to his best and cruised to victory at 8–1 on. The next nearest in the betting was 10–1 against!

It was the same again a month later for the AIG Champion Hurdle at Leopardstown in which Limestone Lad (the only other horse in the betting) was fourth and Theatreworld sixth and last. All three were eight-year-olds (and the remaining three runners were four, five and six). Age was not catching up with Istabraq. He headed off to join Champion Hurdle three-timers, Hatton's

Grace, Sir Ken, Persian War and See You Then. Theatreworld, also trained by Aidan O'Brien, was once more in the line-up.

French Holly had made a blemish-free start to steeplechasing for trainer Ferdy Murphy the previous October, winning by eighteen lengths, but he had then been killed outright – a broken neck in a schooling fall at home, a devastating and most unusual occurrence.

Istabraq's third Smurfit Champion Hurdle was, if anything, even more impressive than his previous two, although he had to survive a pre-race scare when blood was found in his nostril on arrival in England. There was no sign of trouble in the race as Istabraq jumped fluently and 'landed running', relishing each flight and totally in love with the game like the old pro he now was. He beat the five-year-old Hors La Loi III (who was to win the 2002 Champion with Dean Gallagher in the saddle) so easily that he was still 'on the bridle' at the last and simply accelerated clear up that famous hill.

It was Istabraq's twenty-first hurdling win from twenty-four starts. He had finished second in each of the other three, two of them by a head. The prospect of an unprecedented fourth Champion Hurdle looked not only possible but actually probable, and as Istabraq prepared for the feat he was already odds-on favourite. Preparation was not as smooth as in previous years. Appearing on the track later than usual, at the Leopardstown Christmas Festival, he was 4–1 on but may have been a little ring-rusty. It had rained and hailed so hard that the ground was heavy. All main contenders headed to the last as tired horses, with Istabraq a close third. When challenging at the last flight, Istabraq fell, headlong, for the first time in his life. The race went to an up-and-coming youngster, a future dual Queen Mother Champion chaser called Moscow Flyer.

The rumour mill began circulating, but Istabraq redeemed himself next time out when he notched up his fourth consecutive AIG Champion Hurdle at Leopardstown. Again there was drama when this time Moscow Flyer fell at the second-last, but to his countless fans Istabraq looked right back to his best. It was a perfect rehearsal for the Smurfit Champion Hurdle, and the Irish prepared for another riotously happy trip across the water. Moscow Flyer was considered Istabraq's only serious rival for the hurdling crown.

Fate intervened.

Without any premonition or warning, the dreaded foot-and-mouth disease landed like a bolt out of the blue in the north of England and rampaged across the country. While the optimists hoped for a postponement, once the dread disease reached within a certain radius of Cheltenham it was inevitable that the whole meeting be cancelled. A noble substitute meeting was staged at Sandown, but there would be no actual Cheltenham Gold Cup winner of 2001, no Queen Mother Champion Chaser or World Staying Hurdler. Neither was there to be a fourth Champion Hurdle for Istabraq.

To put it in perspective, the real losers were the British farmers who saw whole herds and flocks that they had built up over generations slaughtered and flung onto massive incineration pyres.

By late April some racing had resumed in Ireland. It had not stopped completely in England, but only where a course was within a certain radius of an outbreak – as was Cheltenham. The

Shell Champion Hurdle was held at Leopardstown, taking over from Punchestown, where the ground was deemed unfit for racing. There were seven runners, and Istabraq was his customary odds-on. He looked and felt brilliant, and he came to the last flight with his race won – but, inexplicably, he fell. The beneficiary was, again, Moscow Flyer.

Istabraq reappeared in December when he managed to win the Leopardstown Christmas Festival hurdle by just a head from Bust Out. It was not all that impressive. The now-ten-year-old set off for his final crack at the Champion Hurdle in March. He started favourite, as in the past twenty-seven of his twenty-eight hurdle races, but he was odds-against, at 2–1. The last time he had run when not odds-on was way back in 1998 when he was 3–1 for his first Champion Hurdle.

This time there was to be no fairy tale. Istabraq jumped just two hurdles when, concerned that he did not feel right, Charlie Swan pulled him up before the third. He was found to have pulled a muscle in his back. The race was won by Hors La Loi III, but as Istabraq hacked back past the cheering crowds in the packed grandstands and on the lawn, it sounded as if the Cheltenham roof was going to be lifted sky-high once again – for they realised they had seen one of the sport's greatest hurdlers in action for the last time. Aidan O'Brien recalls, 'He was naturally brilliant; he was intelligent and highly strung. He'd a lot of nervous energy; like most athletes at peak fitness, he liked to be left alone. At his peak, he could walk on a knife edge.'

Istabraq's story continues in retirement. J. P. McManus has long held a policy of keeping his retired horses at home in

Martinstown, Co. Limerick. The 400 acres there house four separate yards, each with a horse-walker, and the horses who go there for their summer holidays invariably return to their trainers fit enough to start cantering. When they retire – however long or short their career has been – they come home to Martinstown. One field is reserved for Cheltenham winners alone!

Istabraq is turned out with the all-conquering 'banks' horse, Risk Of Thunder in a paddock behind J.P.'s magnificent country house. At first he was kept very busy parading at various race meetings, and he still revels in the attention of visitors.

For John Durkan's widow, Carol, there was, in time, happiness in store. She and Istabraq's sole hurdles rider, Charlie Swan, married in July 2006.

Istabraq remains a favourite among racegoers, and they still avidly buy models, portraits, prints, postcards and posters of him. A massive portrait, 13 feet by 10 feet, was painted by Nicola Russell, and unveiled at Punchestown 2011 before being hung in Dublin Airport's T2 from September 2011 until spring 2012.

10

Dorans Pride

For sheer longevity coupled with ability, Dorans Pride was one of Ireland's best-loved chasers from April 1993 to March 2003. In that time he graced the turf the length and breadth of Ireland as well as England's premier tracks, amassing a staggering seventy-six runs (forty-three of them graded), of which he won thirty-three and placed in a further twenty-four. And yet, for many people, his success is bittersweet.

Trainer Michael Hourigan bought the horse, a chestnut gelding by Orchestra out of Marians Pride, from breeders Alfie Buller and Hugh Suffern in Northern Ireland because, 'I trained his dam, which is why I was attracted to him.' Hourigan sold the youngster on to London-based Irishman Tom Doran, and the new owner promptly called him Dorans Pride. For a decade he was the pride of Ireland. He put Michael Hourigan on the map in what was a rocky ride to the ranks of leading trainers, but Hourigan proved he was no one-horse wonder, for following in Dorans Pride's foot-steps came record-breaking ten-time Grade 1 steeplechase win-ner Beef Or Salmon – and a good few other top horses besides.

Dorans Pride was looked after in the stables by Aidan Fitzgerald initially and later by Michael's daughter, Kay. He was nicknamed 'Padjo' by Ros Easom, who was also attached to the Hourigan stables at Lisaleen, a stone's throw from Limerick Race-course at Patrickswell. He proved a 'hardy buck' to break, but on the evening of 19 April 1993 he was ready for his first run. This was at Ballinrobe on the first of its series of summer meetings.

The attractive course in Co. Mayo, like a number of other Irish courses, only races in the summer, it being too wet in the winter. A mix of flat and jumping makes for variety and means that both flat and National Hunt jockeys regularly share a weighing room, but it also means that their racing opportunities per meet-ing are limited, unlike in England where the majority of meetings are all under either one code or the other, so jockeys there can have up to six or more rides per meeting.

Dorans Pride's win on his debut in the bumper at Ballinrobe was a sign of things to come. He was put away for his summer holi-day and next appeared at Listowel in September where he won a maiden hurdle. In January 1994, now officially a five-year-old and teamed up for the first time with Michael Hourigan's stable jockey Shane Broderick, he beat Imperial Call, who was to win the

1996 Cheltenham Gold Cup, by a short head in Naas. Two more wins put him on course for the Sun Alliance Novices Hurdle at the Cheltenham Festival. He was 14–1 in a field of twenty-three and ran a cracker. He was disputing for second place when he fell at the last – an omen, perhaps, of things to come. The winner was Danoli, another who was to become a particular Irish favourite.

The 1994–5 season opened with a win in a Grade 3 hurdle in Navan in November. The following month, Dorans Pride was second behind Danoli in the Hatton's Grace Grade 1 hurdle at Fairyhouse. He beat that horse by a distance in the Christmas Leopardstown meeting. A win at Punchestown's traditional Cheltenham trials day in February put him spot on for another trip across the water for the Stayers (now World) Hurdle.

There was to be no repeat of his fall the previous year, and Dorans Pride swept away the opposition in a manner that impressed many punters and armchair viewers – as well as connections. For Michael Hourigan, who had begun his training career with a couple of horses, it was a truly sweet moment: his first win at the National Hunt Festival. What was more, hurdling was only ever going to be a prelude to steeplechasing for Dorans Pride.

He won twice more over hurdles but, after winning the December 1995 Hatton's Grace Hurdle at Fairyhouse, he went down with a bout of colic, a painful affliction even in light cases. It was so serious that he nearly died. His life was saved on the operating table, but it was to be October of the following year before he was fit enough to race again. That was when he made his steeplechasing bow, and he did it in stupendous style by winning his first five steeplechases in a row.

The racing public, as well as the horse's connections, felt that here was a potential big star, and the Cheltenham Gold Cup, no less, was in their sights. Dorans Pride's first chase was on his local track at Limerick, followed by the Grade 3 Irish Field Novice Chase at Punchestown in October. He beat future Gold Cup winner See More Business twice, in Fairyhouse and Leopardstown, and in between won a Leopardstown Christmas Meeting novice chase by a distance at 5–1 on. Just as his price was shortening for the Cheltenham Gold Cup, he put a blip on his record by falling when in a clear lead at the second-last fence of the Kinloch Brae Chase in Thurles, Co. Tipperary, in February 1997.

The thrill of a lifetime for Shane Broderick came as he lined up for the Gold Cup, and Dorans Pride came home in an honourable third place behind Mr Mulligan; hopes were high that the pair would win the following year.

No one could have foreseen that it would be the young man's last ride on Dorans Pride. Less than three weeks later, at the Irish Grand National meeting in Fairyhouse on 31 March 1997, Shane won a chase and so went out for the 2½-mile handicap chase in buoyant form on board the unfortunately named Another Deadly. There were only eight runners, and his horse was an experienced old pro who he had ridden twice before: back in December 1994 and in the Captain Christy Beginners Chase in January 1996, when the pair had finished fourth of twelve behind Danoli. The Fairyhouse race was Another Deadly's forty-sixth career start during which time he had fallen just once, in December 1992. The crashing fall he took that Easter was to leave his twenty-two-year-old jockey a quadriplegic.

Plate 17   Dorans Pride, with Richard Dunwoody up, jumps the last on his way to victory in the 1998 Hennessy Cognac Gold Cup at Leopardstown.

Plate 18   Dorans Pride with Richard Dunwoody in the 1998 Cheltenham Gold Cup in which they finished third.

Plate 19
Beef Or Salmon, looking magnificent, with trainer's daughter Laura Hourigan, takes in the Aintree scene in April 2006. He ran in the Betfair Bowl Chase on the Melling course, but unseated his rider.

Plate 20 (top)
Timmy Murphy on Beef Or Salmon en route to winning the Punchestown Heineken Gold Cup in April 2004.

Plate 21 (right)
Trainer Michael Hourigan on board Beef Or Salmon during the Racehorse to Riding Horse class at the 2010 Fáilte Ireland Dublin Horse Show.

Plate 22   Moscow Flyer and Barry Geraghty win the Queen Mother Champion Chase, March 2005.

Plate 23   A flying dismount from Barry Geraghty after Moscow Flyer regains the Queen Mother Champion Chase, 2005.

Plate 24   Hardy Eustace with Conor O'Dwyer leads the Champion Hurdle from start to finish at Cheltenham, 16 March 2004.

Plate 25   Hardy Eustace (right), ridden by Conor O'Dwyer, wins from Harchibald (centre) and Brave Inca (left) in an exciting finish to the 2005 Smurfit Champion Hurdle Challenge Trophy.

Plate 26 (left)
Jockey Glen Boss raises his hands in triumph after riding Makybe Diva to win the 2004 Melbourne Cup at Flemington Racecourse. On her left (yellow cap, black silks with yellow stars) is the gallant Vinnie Roe (Pat Smullen) from the Curragh yard of trainer Dermot Weld.

Plate 27 (below)
Makybe Diva wins the Melbourne Cup for a historic third time at Flemington Racecourse, Tuesday, 1 November 2005.

Plate 28 All four feet off the ground, Zenyatta wins the Breeders' Cup Classic at Santa Anita Park, California, November 2009.

Plate 29 Jockey Mike Smith rides Zenyatta to win the Vanity Handicap horse race at Hollywood Park in Inglewood, California, Sunday, 14 June 2010.

Dorans Pride had given the hard-working young man an early taste of racecourse success, and, with a good job as stable jockey to Michael Hourigan, there was every reason, barring accidents, to believe he would become a leading National Hunt rider. The racing world, most of whom would acknowledge 'There but for the grace of God go I', rallied round, and today Shane trains successfully from a wheelchair at his Roscrea, Co. Tipperary, stables, with a winner at the 2011 Listowel Festival, and, most recently as I write, another at the Kilkenny Festival, July 2012. His accident was a reminder, if any were needed, of the dangers facing jockeys, but the adrenalin brought by speed, the thrill of soaring over steeplechase fences on a good jumper and the sheer joy of winning on a finely tuned Thoroughbred outweighs any countenance of such dangers.

The new regular jockey for Dorans Pride became Richard Dunwoody and, in later years, Michael Hourigan's son, Paul. The 1997–8 season was probably the heyday of Dorans Pride. A nine-year-old in 1998, he was in the prime of his life, and he became a popular ante-post favourite months ahead of the Gold Cup, putting up fine performances to win the Kerry National at Listowel in September, the Morris Oil Chase in Clonmel (beating Imperial Call), and a Grade 1 chase at the Fairyhouse December meeting in quick succession. The newspaper correspondents and the public were full of him.

January brought an inexplicable blip when Dorans Pride could finish only fifth of five in a handicap chase at Naas. Only a month later, he was back to his eye-catching best to take the Hennessy Gold Cup at Leopardstown, a perfect prep for Cheltenham, for which he started favourite. There was a surprise winner in store. While Dorans Pride ran his usual gallant race, staying on at the finish to be third again, it was Cool Dawn who stayed in front throughout and took the spoils at 25–1.

Cool Dawn had been bought as a point-to-pointer for Dido Harding, an amateur in the true sense, and she progressed from point-to-points to win two hunter chases on him, as well as finishing second to Enda Bolger on Elegant Lord in the 1996 Cheltenham Foxhunters. When it became clear that he could be even better, he was brought over to Fairyhouse where Conor O'Dwyer rode him into third place in the Irish Grand National. Three wins in Ascot chases in late 1997 and early 1998 (with professional jockey Andrew Thornton now his usual rider) might have shortened his price for the Gold Cup had he not been pulled up in his next race, prior to Cheltenham. On the day, it was Cool Dawn's trophy.

For Dorans Pride, there were to be two more unplaced attempts on the Gold Cup (eighth behind See More Business and sixth to Looks Like Trouble), two more wins in the Morris Oil Chase at Clonmel and another Ericsson in December 1998, when the favourite, Florida Pearl, fell three out, leaving the three-years-older Dorans Pride to win by a distance.

Michael Hourigan had more surprises to spring with his now veteran. In March 1999, shortly after his Gold Cup eighth, Dorans Pride lined up for the 2-mile Kildare flat race on the Curragh where, in the hands of Jamie Spencer, he won. In January 2000, Paul Hourigan steered him to win a listed handicap hurdle in Navan. In September 2000, he turned out to win a charity flat race with Tommy Carberry and, without doubt, a lot of lead on his back to make up the weight to 12 stone 4 pounds. And then, possibly his finest feat of all, Dorans Pride won the 2000 Leopardstown November Handicap, ridden by Niall McCullagh at the advanced flat racer's age of eleven. He was by far the oldest horse in the race, and he beat the Mick Kinane-ridden favourite. For almost his entire career Dorans Pride had been a National Hunt racer so his experience on the flat was minimal.

The following week it was back to jumping, and he was second to Looks Like Trouble in the James Nicholson Chase, Down Royal. The week after that he turned out to win the Morris Oil Chase at Clonmel for a stunning fourth successive year. It was a great achievement, and it was to be his last win under rules. He still loved his work, and for the remainder of that 2000–1 season he was consistently placed: third in the Hatton's Grace Hurdle, second to Rince Ri in the Ericsson, third to Florida Pearl in the Hennessy and three more thirds, often carrying top weight.

He ran twice at the Royal Ascot meeting of June 2001 where he finished a gallant third in the 2½-mile Queen Alexandra Stakes. That November he ran again in a listed hurdle in Navan (and was fourth of five), and the following April he finished eighth of twenty in the At the Races Gold Cup (better known as the Whitbread/Bet365).

Dorans Pride was thirteen years old, and his speed was dented – though not his love of the game. It was time to retire, but the horse had other ideas. He loathed being idle. All he wanted was to come back in and be part of the string again. Pow-wows were held to decide what would be best for him. Perhaps he could doddle round a few point-to-points?

In January and February 2003, Dorans Pride ran in three open point-to-points and won them all, relishing his new role. At fourteen years of age, he was clearly rejuvenated. A second in the Raymond Smith Memorial Hunter Chase at Leopardstown and the old boy was allowed to go back one more time to Cheltenham, to contest the Foxhunters – the 'amateurs Gold Cup' for point-to-pointers and hunter chasers only.

Michael Hourigan had three runners on Thursday, 13 March 2003, and (dreams being free) dreamed of bringing home three winners. It is hard to imagine a day as awful for a trainer. All three of his horses fell: Hi Cloy, a 50–1 shot in the Royal and Sun Alliance Novices Hurdle (won by Hardy Eustace); new kid on the block Beef Or Salmon, 5–1 second favourite in the Gold Cup; and Dorans Pride in the Foxhunters. At only the second fence of the course he knew so well, Dorans Pride fell and broke a hind leg. There was no alternative but to put the old friend down. Michael Hourigan says, 'He chose the scene himself. He hated being retired and would have wasted away. He died doing what he did best – but it was a big cross to carry. I felt so sorry for my wife, Anne, and for my daughter, Kay, who looked after him.'

A horse like Dorans Pride – a horse of a lifetime – is hard to follow, but for Michael Hourigan there was Beef Or Salmon, and in autumn 2011 Tom Doran once again had his colours carried to victory by Clear Hills. The trainer was Michael Hourigan, and the venue the four-year-old maiden at the point-to-point at Rathcannon, Co. Limerick. Champion point-to-point rider Derek O'Connor kept the horse, a bay by Marju, handy, led before the last and won 'snugly' according to the form book. Certainly it was good enough to believe that the Doran colours may once again grace the big tracks in the not-too-distant future.

11

Beef Or Salmon

A great favourite with the Irish, Beef Or Salmon should be remembered for winning ten Grade 1 chases (a record at the time) and not for failing in all five attempts at the Cheltenham Gold Cup. Perhaps he was just a home-loving boy, but probably more influential was the horrific fall he took in his first Cheltenham Gold Cup, as a seven-year-old in 2003.

Beef Or Salmon crashed at the third fence, the one away from the stands; he rolled over and thumped onto the ground a second time, and then, yet again. It was a miracle he wasn't killed – as was Dorans Pride, in a much simpler fall, in the very next race. Even more to his credit is that he went on, after prolonged treatment by back specialist Liz Kent and physiotherapist Sue Shortt, and intense care from his devoted lass Kay Hourigan (Michael's daughter), to win the races in Ireland that he did.

Michael Hourigan had an equine swimming pool, and there is no doubt that this provided therapy for Beef Or Salmon. Michael also liked to box his horses up and bring them to nearby Beale Beach or to the banks of the Shannon, where they enjoyed not only a change of scene but also paddling in the salt water, an added benefit. Salmon was able to keep on racing, but the work of his human therapists continued.

Unfashionably bred, it was to Beef Or Salmon's good fortune that he was trained by Michael Hourigan. Hourigan's path to the ranks of leading trainers was not a smooth one. From a non-horsey family, as a kid he loved nothing more than to hang around the local stables – often in preference to going to school. As soon as he was old enough to leave formal education, at the age of fourteen, he was apprenticed to Charlie Weld (Dermot's father) on the Curragh. During his five years there, Michael rode nine winners.

He followed with a spell jumping (winning a chase and three hurdles) but says that he wasn't cut out for it. At the age of twenty-five and newly married, he took out a trainer's licence. He had no land, let alone facilities, and trained his first few horses from the back of a pub and in various back gardens around the village of Rathkeale in Co. Limerick, supplementing his meagre income by lorry driving. His first winner came in 1979. In 1985 he moved to his current site at Lisaleen, Co. Limerick, when it was bare fields with one tiny cottage, and he has been steadily building it up ever since, helped by Dorans Pride's 1994 win at the Cheltenham Festival.

Beef Or Salmon was bred by John Murphy of Wexford, who used a little-known American-bred stallion called Cajetano, who stood way up in Co. Meath at Williamstown Stud, Clonee. He had won six races and placed nineteen times when trained by Jack Barbe. Cajetano is an Italian boy's name, meaning 'from Gaeta'. Cajetano was bred by Nelson Bunker Hunt, American oil magnate and disgraced silver marketeer, and owner-breeder of renown with such as Dahlia (the Irish Oaks, two King George and Queen Elizabeth Stakes, the Canadian International, the Washington DC International and group races in France) and 1976 Epsom Derby winner Empery. Cajetano was by Run the Gantlet, and his third sire was Ribot, one of the all-time greats and winner of all sixteen of his races in the 1950s, including two Prix de l'Arc de Triomphes.

Cajetano was despatched to stud in Italy after standing for about three seasons in Ireland in the mid-1990s. Such is the lot of some sires without well-known progeny – or, in the case of National Hunt horses, whose progeny have not had time to prove themselves on the track.

Cajetano sired only two known winners from a believed five racehorses. Besides Beef Or Salmon, Dark Crusader won two races, but Blue Flu – also trained by Michael Hourigan – had such little success, it has to be said, that it's a wonder Hourigan considered buying another horse by the same sire. His eye said yes, and his eye was right. He gives that little smile, a slight shrug of the shoulders and the trademark twinkle in the eye when asked about it.

Cajetano had better success siring show jumpers. In May 2011, for example, Ireland's Captain David O'Brien was successful in Hagen, Germany, with Kiltoom, by Cajetano out of Ashley Green.

The mating that produced Beef Or Salmon was with a mare called Farinella, who was by Salmon Leap, which seems to be where the chestnut colour comes in, and he was by the great Northern Dancer. Farinella was out of a Bold Lad mare, Boldella, who produced four winners and was herself well related to Group 2 winners in France, Ireland and America – so to someone prepared to look hard enough, the pedigree was there. Farinella gave birth to a chestnut colt on 30 April 1996. She died in 2000, a year before her only famous racing son made his racecourse debut.

John Murphy sold the now gelding in August 1999 as an unbroken three-year-old. He made a modest 5,400 guineas at Tattersalls to a cash buyer, but the chestnut was back in the ring the following June, consigned by Emer Berry for the Goffs Land Rover Sale, where Michael Hourigan bought him for £6,500.

It was not all plain sailing in the early days of Beef Or Salmon. He proved easy and straightforward to break and was a natural athlete, but no one seemed to want to buy him. An unfashionable sire might have been part of the reason for that. It is usual for a trainer to sell on his newly acquired young stock, in the hope that the new owner will keep it in his yard for training.

Three times the Hourigans thought they had found an owner for him, and three times the sale failed to go through, at asking prices of £10,000, £12,000 and £15,000. Apparently, one of those customers decided that the trainer was trying to make too much profit on his purchase price, but in the intervening time, of course, much hard work had been put into breaking, schooling and preparing the youngster for racing. Not only that, they now had him ready to run in a point-to-point, and he had shown enough at home for them to think he might win.

Along came prospective purchasers number four: Joe Craig and Dan McLarnon from Northern Ireland. The asking price was now £30,000 plus £5,000 each for his first point-to-point and bumper wins.

Point-to-pointing in Ireland looks, at first glance, similar to the sport in England: farmland with a roped-off track or marker flags, birch (or increasingly plastic) fences, a paddock erected by chestnut palings, changing tents for the jockeys, a line of bookmakers, a beer tent and rows of horse boxes, trailers and cars. Scrutiny of the race card reveals the difference: the UK will have a variety of races open to all ages and will include a maiden, but in Ireland the majority of races are maidens, and they are much more specific: four-year-olds only, five- and six-year-old mares, seven- and eight-year-old geldings and all the various permutations, but very few races for older horses. The reason is that in Ireland point-to-pointing is more of a shop window for breeders and producers. Almost every horse running will be for sale, and after a horse wins it is not uncommon to see prospective purchasers holding their chequebooks in the lorry area. In the UK, licensed trainers are not allowed to run horses in point-to-points (although they can in hunter chases), but Irish trainers can and do run horses in point-to-points as part of their education – and to show them off to prospective purchasers, many of whom will be English.

On 28 January 2001, Beef Or Salmon was a street clear at the final fence of his first point-to-point at Dungarvan when he fell, but three weeks later he made no such mistake and readily collected at the meeting near Clonmel to put the first of twenty career wins on the slate, winning by a distance in the sixteen-runner field.

That was the first £5,000 contingency for Messrs Craig and McLarnon to stump up. They did not have long to wait for the second. After a creditable third of twenty-seven in the Goffs Land Rover bumper at Punchestown, Salmon won on his next outing, a bumper at Clonmel. That concluded the owners' purchasing commitments – and the unfashionably bred Beef Or Salmon went on to earn a career total of just under £1 million (£985,658 under rules plus a point-to-point).

Beef Or Salmon also fell in his first hurdle race, a maiden at nearby Limerick, when odds-on. He soon made amends, winning another bumper at Cork and then opening his hurdling account at Gowran Park. He wasn't a brilliant hurdler, and at the start of the next season, 2002–3, Michael Hourigan decided to send him chasing. He bypassed the usual novice route and put him straight in against seasoned chasers. The advantage was that he wouldn't be surrounded by big fields of 'novice' beginners with the inherent risks of being crossed, knocked into or brought down. The danger was that he might be taken off his legs by the older pros.

First, Michael ran him in two flat races. His daughter, Laura, rode him in the first, winning a qualified riders race at Galway in October by eleven lengths. He then ran in the November Handicap, the race that Dorans Pride had won two years previously in his twilight years. Beef Or Salmon did his best to emulate his stable companion, finishing third (promoted to second) of seventeen, carrying only 7 stone 13 pounds on his back. Michael Hourigan knew Salmon had the speed all right. And he also knew he had the jumping ability – not only from his point-to-point venture but also from extensive schooling at home. He lifted himself over the fences and got away from them quickly, an ideal combination for a steeplechaser.

And so it was off to the 2½-mile Grade 2 Morris Oil Chase at Clonmel, Co. Tipperary, in November 2002, the race that Dorans Pride had won four times. By this time there was a lot of press and public interest in the young horse and his unorthodox career route. If his trainer thought he could go directly into a Grade 2 open chase, surely he must be something special.

Beef Or Salmon was up against four seasoned and useful campaigners. Nine-year-old Sackville had won sixteen races, nine of them chases, and his stable companion, ten-year-old Moscow Express, also trained by Frances Crowley (flat jockey Pat Smullen's wife) had won twenty-three races, including that race the previous year. In between he had run in the Cheltenham Gold Cup. Cregg House, aged seven, had three wins on the slate for trainer Paddy Mullins, and the favourite was the eight-year-old Mouse Morris-trained Alcapone who had to that day been first past the post five times.

Beef Or Salmon had a weight of 10 stone 13 pounds including star jockey Paul Carberry on his back and was receiving some weight from his rivals. The fact that his four rivals had already won forty-seven races between them made not a tad of difference to Beef Or Salmon. It was a copybook Paul Carberry ride, tracking the others and jumping superbly, getting his mount's confidence with no fear of interference around him. And then that downhill sweep at Clonmel, easing through into contention. Sackville took over the lead from Alcapone at the second-last, where the favourite unseated Barry Geraghty, but they looked held at the time. Salmon was on the leader's heels, and as he faced the uphill stretch and the final fence, Carberry let out his reins a notch, cleared the last fence and drew clear to win unextended, with Sackville a respectful three and a half lengths behind.

Ireland truly had a new steeplechasing talent to talk about.

It was a roller-coaster ride from there. Wins against the very best that Ireland had to offer set tongues wagging: the Grade 3 Hilly Way Chase at Cork with Timmy Murphy up, and then on to his first Grade 1, the 3-mile Ericsson Chase at Leopardstown's Christmas meeting – it was only his third-ever steeplechase. Timmy Murphy continued what was to become Beef Or Salmon's trademark: settle in at the rear of the field, move smoothly forwards two out, lead at the last and run on strongly. On this occasion the useful Colonel Braxton was behind him, with the favourite, the French star First Gold, last of seven. Six weeks later, Salmon repeated the dose to Colonel Braxton, Harbour Pilot and Rince Ri on the same course for the Hennessy Cognac Gold Cup, with Florida Pearl pulling up.

The rookie steeplechaser had beaten the best chasers that Ireland had to offer. Cheltenham was the next port of call. Why go for one of the novice chases when your horse has already beaten some regular Gold Cup contenders? There have been other novice Gold Cup winners such as Dawn Run, who was eight, and seven-year-old Captain Christie, but inevitably some failures as well. Owners and trainer consulted, but really there was only ever going to be one answer: go for the Gold Cup.

After the Gold Cup, where, as we have seen, he took that sickening fall, Beef Or Salmon next ran in a flat race and then bypassed the Punchestown Festival altogether. In the 2-mile Kildare flat race on the Curragh he was ridden by no less a man than Mick Kinane. If ever proof were needed of Michael Hourigan's empathy with his horses it was this move. There were twenty-eight runners, but Beef Or Salmon ran out the winner – as good a confidence-restorer as could be imagined.

Salmon then went off for his well-deserved summer break, returning for Clonmel the following November. He was favourite but made a bad mistake at the last fence to finish third to Edredon Bleu. His career became something of a see-saw, winning numerous Grade 1 chases, interspersed with jumping errors – but although these sometimes cost him a race, never again did he fall (although just once he unseated his rider).

To the racing public, especially those in his native Ireland, he became much loved but also exasperating. It wasn't always jumping errors: in his first, eagerly anticipated contest with Best Mate at Leopardstown, on the back of Hilly Way and John Durkan Chase wins, his run was lack-lustre. He was found to be ill; it knocked him back so much that he was unable to reappear at the next big Leopardstown meeting. He recovered in time for the Gold Cup and had his best result in that race, finishing fourth to Best Mate, who galloped into history with his third successive win, the first to do so since Arkle nearly forty years before. There were many who felt Beef Or Salmon had a future Gold Cup in him, especially when he landed the Heineken Gold Cup at the Punchestown Festival next time out.

Would he finally find his full glory in the 2004–5 season? The see-saw began going up and down again. Salmon beat Kicking King at Down Royal in November but then that future Gold Cup winner beat him in Punchestown. Next up was the Leopardstown Christmas meeting with its highlight, the Lexus (formerly Ericsson) Chase, and one horse was expected to win: Best Mate. The appearance of the triple Gold Cup winner ensured that crowds flocked to the south Dublin track.

What an exhilarating race it proved to be. For once Salmon was 'underdog' as Best Mate started a shade odds-on favourite. As usual, Beef Or Salmon was held up at the rear of the six-runner field. Best Mate, with Irish jockey Jim Culloty up, made a mistake at the first fence. As others dropped away, Best Mate moved up into third place with less than a mile to run and took second at the penultimate – but Beef Or Salmon had cruised into the lead from his usual place at the rear on the previous fence. There was an audible murmur in the packed stands. Could the Irish-trained horse really bring it off? By two fences from home he had put daylight between himself and his pursuers. At the last fence, spectators held their collective breaths. (Please don't go and make one of your mistakes now!) The chestnut was foot perfect, flawless over the final fence, where Rule Supreme, alongside Best Mate, fell.

As Beef Or Salmon set off up the run-in, his short tail stuck out behind him, the irrepressible Paul Carberry had a long look round in the saddle. Best Mate was toiling in his wake, and Paul cheekily beckoned him to 'Come on and catch me!' It was done in jest, but it didn't go down too well in some official quarters. The horse's fans, however, went wild and gave him a rapturous, cheering welcome.

Best Mate was to have just one more race in his remarkable life: the following November on his seasonal appearance at Exeter. He pulled up, collapsed when walking back and died. Apart from the loss of a wonderful horse, one of the saddest things was to see him start that race as an unconsidered outsider, with six of the eleven runners at shorter odds. Before that day, his record stood at fourteen wins and seven seconds from all his runs.

Beef Or Salmon's career probably reached its peak that day at Leopardstown, but he was not done yet, even though the Willie Mullins-trained Rule Supreme beat him next time in the Hennessy at Leopardstown, and he pulled up in his third attempt at the Gold Cup, behind Kicking King.

With both the Lexus and the Hennessy going to him, Salmon proved he was no back number, beating War of Attrition and Hedgehunter respectively. In 2006, with multiple Grade 1 races like the Hennessy Gold Cup, Lexus Chase and Heineken Gold Cup safely under his belt, it was no surprise that the popular chestnut with the distinctive short tail was ante-post favourite for that year's Cheltenham Gold Cup. His delightful owners, Joe Craig and Dan McLarnon, hoped to have his book written should he win. Hopes were high that he could at last overcome his Gold Cup jinx. It was not to be. Cheltenham and Beef Or Salmon didn't suit each other, and that year's glory went to another Irish-trained and owned horse, War of Attrition, while Beef Or Salmon trailed in eleventh of the twenty-two runners, an unusually big Gold Cup field.

Expectations were not so high the following season although Beef Or Salmon retained a steady base of fans. He showed all his strength of character in the James Nicholson Chase at Down

Royal, where, in an amazing finish, he beat the Gold Cup hero by a neck. As ever, he could beat Gold Cup winners, but not in the Gold Cup.

Bidding for a fourth Lexus at Christmas, Beef Or Salmon couldn't beat England's grey, The Listener. Yet, over the same course and distance for the Hennessy a few weeks later, and fitted with blinkers for the first time, Beef Or Salmon produced as courageous a performance as ever. The Listener had, as usual, set up a long lead and was odds-on to repeat his success, but Beef Or Salmon, and his now regular partner Andrew McNamara, refused to give in.

They set off up the run-in so far behind the leader that not even the most optimistic spectator could believe he could reel him in. It didn't look as if he was making any impression. And then, somehow, that inherent class, coupled with Beef Or Salmon's own indomitable will, saw him surge forward. Even a few lengths before the line it didn't look possible – but he did it: he drew level with The Listener and powered to a three-quarters of a length win. Once more the cheers threatened to lift the roof off the grandstand, and staid middle-age racegoers ran round the back to welcome him into the winner's enclosure.

It was to be his last win but, true to himself, he did it in style.

For his fifth and final attempt at the Gold Cup, different tactics were tried, letting him jump off in front to see if he could enjoy the place better that way, but he faded to finish unplaced behind Kauto Star. He ran for one more season, but in 2008 Michael Hourigan, judiciously, did not even enter him for the Gold Cup. He did have his first attempt at the Irish Grand National, with inevitable top weight, but he couldn't see out the marathon with that weight and was pulled up. After that there was just one more run for the now-twelve-year-old. His swan song was the Guinness Gold Cup at Punchestown in front of his adoring home crowd who gave him a cheer as he passed the post a long way behind the winner, Neptune Collonges (winner four years later of the 2012 Aintree Grand National). It had been a long and honourable – if sometimes erratic – career that stamped itself on the memory of the racing public.

In August 2010 Beef Or Salmon took part in the Racehorse to Riding Horse class at the Dublin Horse Show, with a smiling Michael Hourigan himself in the saddle – but it was won by none other than his old rival War of Attrition.

12

Moscow Flyer

One of the most exciting things for a racing spectator is to stand beside a steeplechase fence during a 2-mile chase. The speed at which the top 2-milers take on 4½ feet of stout birch leaves no room for error and is truly breathtaking to watch. Moscow Flyer was one of the swiftest crossers of a steeplechase fence, and it is hard to disagree with those who rate him the greatest 2-mile chaser of all – and there have been some good ones.

He did, of course, have a flaw, but I think that made us love him all the more. On a number of occasions, thousands of hearts were in thousands of mouths as he 'got one wrong' and ejected

Barry Geraghty like a jet pilot from a crashing plane, sometimes falling himself.

Until he was eleven years old, Moscow Flyer remained undefeated in all his completed steeplechases, a staggering nineteen of them, and when, finally, he was beaten, in front of his home crowd at the 2005 Punchestown National Hunt Festival, he went down fighting, giving way by the shortest of margins. In fact, a strong case can be made that the race was a dead heat, as there was no mirror image for the camera.

By that time his falls were a thing of the past but he set up an extraordinary sequence of three wins followed by a fall or unseat in the early years of his chasing career. And then the penny dropped. He remained the fastest over fences at 2 miles, and with his new-found maturity and sure-footedness he went from April 2004 to April 2005 with seven magical wins in a row.

Moscow Flyer's career was a roller-coaster ride for his connections. New owner Brian Kearney, trainer Jessie Harrington, jockey Barry Geraghty and 'lad' Eamon Leigh (who did the hands-on training before bloodstock agent Johnny Harrington married Jessie) can be forgiven for walking, talking, sleeping and dreaming Moscow Flyer almost to exclusion of anything else for more than seven scintillating, heart-stopping, memorable years. Of course, for Jessie and Barry, and Eamon too, there were other horses to be taken into consideration, but for that period they lived the Moscow dream.

The Dual Champion 2-Mile Chaser might have been called Moscow Max, for that was his new owner's first choice of name (in honour of his grandson), but it was turned down. He might have been a Champion Hurdler but for missing the foot-and-mouth year, and, equally, given his breeding, he might have been a Cheltenham Gold Cup winner. He was bred in Meelick, Co. Clare, by Edward Joyce, who put his unraced mare, Meelick Lady, to Moscow Society, a relatively unknown but well-bred stallion by Nijinsky. Joyce had previously sold his home-bred stock privately, but he entered the horse in the prestigious Tattersalls Derby Sales at Fairyhouse as an unbroken four-year-old in June 1998. His pedigree lacked 'black type' (winners of graded or listed races) in its recent history, and the breeder was relatively unknown. The bright bay with white star and stripe was allotted a late slot on the second and final day, not an ideal position. Two things helped: Jim Mernagh, who 'prepped' him for the sale, kept nagging Johnny Harrington, Jessie's husband, to at least look at him. And Jessie had a would-be owner, Brian Kearney, to buy for, who had an upper limit of £20,000. After failing to buy two horses that made too much money for their prospective new owner, and after finally being persuaded to look at Moscow Flyer and then returning to his box many times, liking him and his athletic model more with each viewing, the horse who was to win well over £1 million in prize money was bought for 17,000 guineas.

His success was not immediate – far from it – and he failed to win so much as a modest bumper. At home he was always a like-able character, and his conformation, stance and general outlook were much admired. He wasn't big but he had presence. He was a quick learner and took only two weeks to break, but he was also capable of 'dropping' his rider, usually with a big buck, just for the fun of it. The more he progressed, the bigger became the hopes

– and the deeper the disappointment in his bumpers. He was tried in bumpers that were slightly longer than the usual 2 miles, the belief being that he was bred to stay, but with the benefit of hindsight it was simply physical immaturity that was holding him back.

When he came back in from his 1999 summer at grass, he was not only bigger and burlier from feasting on the lush 'Dr Green', but he was also noticeably stronger. Jessie told his owner not to despair. Friends had warned Kearney before his venture into ownership not to think of it as an investment, but naturally he yearned for the thrill of seeing his black and white (for Belvedere College) colours come home in front.

Jessie Harrington was comparatively new to the training ranks but she had a lifelong experience of horses. She represented Ireland in three-day eventing. She felt Moscow Flyer should win a bumper. They took him to a schooling bumper, which he won easily, having had an altercation with a marker post in the earlier schooling hurdle race. Barry Geraghty was left on the ground after just three flights – but Moscow Flyer had jumped them perfectly.

A stone bruise prevented him running in the planned bumper, and so, after all, he began the season in an eleven-runner maiden hurdle, against an odds-on chance, the Noel Meade-trained Young Buck ridden by Paul Carberry. Young Buck had won a bumper impressively, but, try as he did, he couldn't land a blow against Moscow Flyer, who drew clear by three lengths. So it was win number one for Moscow Flyer, in a 2-mile maiden hurdle worth £3,696 at Punchestown on 31 October 1999, Barry Geraghty up. Brian Kearney saw his colours first past the post at last. Like catching your first fish, few moments can match it.

In his next two hurdles, including the Grade 1 Royal Bond at Fairyhouse in late November, Moscow Flyer also beat odds-on favourites. Three from three. He was then given a rest prior to a planned crack at one of the top novice hurdles at Cheltenham. Fate intervened: a niggling lameness behind, and a scan revealed he had a hairline fracture of the pelvis. After box rest, horse-walker sessions and a return to fitness, he went to a Grade 3, 2½-mile hurdle at Fairyhouse. He had been off the course for five months and was electric – but in the wrong way. He got so buzzed up, after his long break, that he was difficult to saddle, impossible to mount in the paddock (he was led out to the course) and then pulled Barry's arms out in the race, until Barry allowed him to go on. That didn't work: the horse expended his pent-up energy too early, and, when his bubble burst, Barry allowed him to coast home, finishing last – the only time in his career he ever did so.

Nine days later, the edge taken off him, Moscow Flyer romped home in the Grade 1 Evening Herald Novice Hurdle at the Punchestown Festival. His starting price was a massive 10–1, and Noel Meade's Sauselito Bay, who had beaten a then-unknown Best Mate in the Supreme Novices Hurdle in Cheltenham, was odds-on. But the race was all about Moscow. Reputation restored, dreams renewed – and off for his summer holiday.

The next season saw him win the Grade 1 AIB Agri-business December Festival Hurdle at Leopardstown when Istabraq fell at the final flight. The following month, at Leopardstown for the AIG Europe Champion Hurdle, the tables were reversed: Moscow Flyer fell at the second-last when just leading from Istabraq, who duly won. That would have been the score between them had the Smurfit Champion Hurdle been held at Cheltenham in March 2001.

Brian Kearney's dream of having a Cheltenham runner was thwarted for the second year when the whole meeting was called off because of foot-and-mouth. It was during the heyday of Istabraq, but Moscow Flyer was the most serious rival for him that year. They were to meet one more time, in the April 2001 Shell Champion Hurdle at Leopardstown (replacing Punchestown due to ground problems there). It looked like Istabraq's race until, again, he fell at the last flight, leaving the spoils to Moscow Flyer. It was Moscow's final hurdle race. Owner and trainer agreed that he would embark on a chasing career the following season.

He schooled well – brilliantly – at home and in racecourse schooling sessions, but come the day, 24 October 2001, in a beginners chase at Fairyhouse and odds-on favourite, he fell. He behaved sensibly during the early part of the race but then attacked two fences in a row as if they were hurdles. He nearly fell the first time and took a cruncher at the next. He was lucky not to be injured (as was Barry), and it probably taught him a lesson. Indeed, he made no such mistake in his next run when romping away with a beginners chase in Down Royal. Or at a Grade 3 novice chase at Punchestown. Or at a Grade 1 novice chase at Leopardstown over Christmas.

Now Brian Kearney could truly dream of a runner – a winner! – at Cheltenham. First there was the Grade 1 Baileys Arkle Novice Chase at Leopardstown in January 2002. Barry Geraghty was sidelined through injury, and Paul Moloney, who had won a hurdle race on Moscow Flyer before, deputised. The opposition was weak enough, and, on paper, all he had to do was jump round, but Moscow, pulling hard, fell at the fifth fence. It was actually the last time he ever fell himself, but some future jumping errors were to give his jockey no chance of staying in the saddle.

So they were off to Cheltenham on the back of a fall. As a result, three of the runners for the Irish Independent Arkle Challenge Trophy Chase were at shorter prices, with Martin Pipe's Seebald, ridden by Tony McCoy, favourite. The Arkle is seen as a pointer to future Queen Mother Champion Chasers, and Moscow Flyer won it in the style of a good 'un, with no jumping errors.

Equally, he won his last race of the season at Punchestown easily, and the first of the next at Down Royal. When he went to Sandown in December 2002 to contest the Tingle Creek, named after one of the most exciting chasers of yesteryear, it was hoped to prove that he could be a serious Queen Mother Champion Chase contender. Ahead of him, Flagship Uberalles, the reigning Champion Chaser, stumbled so badly that Moscow, quick as a flash, jinked sideways to avoid cannoning into him. Poor Barry went straight on into space – and so the dreaded 'UR' (unseated rider) was lodged in the form book.

Two more wins, at Leopardstown (in desperately heavy ground) and at Punchestown, put him bang on track for the Queen Mother. Although the Gold Cup, run over 3¼ miles on the last day of the Festival, is the number-one race in the calendar, the Champion Chase comes close behind, and because it is run over 2 miles the pace is always fast; there is no margin for error in the jumping department.

Eleven lined up for the contest, and three of them fell, two at the penultimate fence when giving do-or-die performances. One was Moscow's old rival, Seebald, and the other was an outsider who ran a cracker, Latalomne. Races are more nerve-wracking for the connections who are watching their horse run than they are for the rider, who is concentrating on his job and probably, as in this case, relishing every moment: Barry Geraghty and Moscow Flyer looked in no danger and stormed up the run-in to claim the great prize.

Not surprisingly, Moscow Flyer was odds-on favourite for the BMW Chase in front of his now legion of fans on his home ground at Punchestown in late May. He jumped into the lead four out and put himself a few lengths clear of his rivals on the home turn two out, where Flagship Uberalles got within a length. Then he hit the fence so low that Barry Geraghty was flying, horseless, through the air.

In the autumn and winter of 2003/4, at the start of the new season, Navan, the Tingle Creek at Sandown and Leopardstown added three more impressive wins to his record. No wonder he went to Cheltenham in defence of his crown at odds-on.

There was just one young pretender in the field, the seven-year-old Azertyuiop. The remaining seven runners were aged between nine and eleven; Moscow was one of the ten-year-olds. One of the things Moscow Flyer had demonstrated over the course of his career was that no matter how good he was – and he was now unbeaten in all twelve chases that he had completed – he occasionally 'got one wrong' and, at 2-mile pace (which is about 35 mph; the 3-mile chasers usually gallop at about 30 mph) that could end his race. If ever it were needed, Moscow Flyer was living proof that there is no such thing as a racing certainty. It happened this time at the open ditch at the top of the hill, four fences from home. Moscow was going seemingly beautifully when he got it totally wrong, had his front feet in the ditch and landed with his nose on the ground. Somehow he didn't fall, but Geraghty was gone, sliding along the ground.

It is to the credit of all the connections that a year later, at the age of eleven, Moscow Flyer redeemed himself. Indeed, he never again lost his jockey in a race. He ran twice more that season after the Champion Chase, winning the Martell Cognac Melling Chase at Aintree, where he stepped up to 2½ miles, and Punchestown's Champion Chase.

When he returned from his summer break in autumn 2004, he was acting better than ever, and so it proved: he won the Fortria Chase at Navan for the second year, the Tingle Creek at Sandown again (beating, significantly, Azertyuiop) and the Tied Cottage Chase at Punchestown at the end of January.

Next stop, Cheltenham. The 2005 Queen Mother Champion Chase had eight runners, and it was a markedly younger field than before. The young pretender this time was Well Chief, only six years old. Four of the others, including Azertyuiop, were eight. There was a ten-year-old and two elevens, including Moscow. With the scintillating form he had been showing, he was 6–4 favourite, followed by the previous year's winner on 2–1 and Well Chief on 7–2. The remainder were 'out with the washing'. Bar a heart-stopping moment at the fourth-last, his bogey fence, Moscow showed much younger legs the way home, to beat Well Chief by an easy two lengths. Some way behind, Azertyuiop was the best of the rest. It was a truly remarkable achievement from Moscow Flyer, leaving many lovers of horse racing with moist eyes.

His seventh consecutive win came when taking the 2½-mile Aintree race again. None watching could have guessed it was to be his last steeplechase win. It was on to his usual seasonal finale in front of his home crowd at Punchestown. Beaten so narrowly – if not actually a dead heat – by Rathgar Beau, it was the beginning of the end for the great horse who, at eleven years of age, had won back the speed-chasing crown.

His was one of the great comebacks, previously only achieved by Edward Courage's brilliantly named Royal Relief (by Flush Royal) back in 1974, and emulated in the 2010 Cheltenham Gold Cup by Kauto Star.

The following autumn, Central House got the better of Moscow in the Fortria Chase in Navan. After that second placing, it was fourth in Leopardstown and fifth in the Queen Mother. Time to call it a day. But there was to be one more surprise. Over the years, it had become a Harrington family joke that, if she was old enough, youngest daughter Kate could ride Moscow Flyer in the annual charity flat race at Punchestown after he retired. Thirteen months after his last chase, and now aged thirteen, Moscow Flyer and Kate, by then eighteen, teamed up for her first taste of race-riding. There were twenty-five runners, twenty-three of them starting at odds of between 10–1 and 33–1. Noel Meade had a runner on 4–1, and Moscow, incredibly, was evens favourite.

Jessica recalls, 'It was the most scary thing I ever did, because if it had gone wrong we were on a hiding to nothing.' Moscow's class belied his years, and he and his rookie jockey did nothing wrong, showing a clean pair of heels to all their rivals. It was the perfect swansong.

Moscow Flyer wasn't big for a chaser, but he was beautifully made, on a model not unlike Red Rum and with similar qualities of athleticism. But, as with Red Rum, there was more to it. From the outside it is hard to tell a good 'un from a horse who will prove moderate. We can't see inside, to the heart, to the lungs or – in particular – to the spirit. Therein lies the secret to success.

For Brian Kearney there were to be a few more racehorses. Just one of them managed to win a race – once only. Jessica's skill has seen her advance up the flat training ranks in addition to joining the elite of National Hunt trainers. And Barry Geraghty, building on his success, was appointed stable jockey to Nicky Henderson in Lambourn in 2008.

As for Moscow Flyer, he lives a life of pampered luxury. He went first to the Irish Horse Welfare Trust (IHWT), which, as its name suggests, cares for mistreated, neglected or abandoned horses and ponies, and so at first sight it seems an anomaly that Moscow Flyer was sent there for his retirement. After all, no horse on the planet could have been better cared for than Moscow Flyer. Then the eye notices the list of IHWT patrons, and amongst them is Jessica Harrington; there lies the clue. The presence of Moscow Flyer lifts the charity's profile, makes the public more aware of its work. He is the IHWT's flagship. More than that, in truth, he is its principal patron.

Moscow Flyer enjoyed being kingpin at the IHWT headquarters in Woodenbridge, Co. Wicklow, where he loved nothing more than to pose for visitors' cameras or to give them a nudge for a titbit. For their part, the members of staff loved having him. Their devotion and dedication to some desperate cases shines through; their work is nothing short of vocation.

More recently, Moscow Flyer has joined two other Irish racing legends, Vintage Crop and Florida Pearl, at the Irish National Stud, vacating his IHWT stable to one in greater need. Moscow is now much closer to his adoring fans, who can see him whenever they visit the Stud (and its Japanese Gardens), and he, in turn, will draw even more people to what is already one of Ireland's most popular visitor attractions. There, he continues to fly the flag as equine ambassador for the IHWT.

There is much more awareness today for the need of a life after the track for racehorses, in addition to the welfare of all horses and ponies. Thoroughbreds are not a ride for everybody, but there is nothing like the feeling of joy that riding one can give. There are some Thoroughbreds who need no retraining at all, but they are the exception. Others are difficult to break, 'spooky', skittish and capable of giving a big buck (and it won't come with a warning). When they are racing fit, some Thoroughbreds will pull hard, but that is generally in the slower paces at home. With the greater speed of a race (or in a hunter trial, say, for a cob), hard pulling is comparatively rare because the horse is going at a greater speed than at home and has more to concentrate on. The majority of handlers manage to train most racehorses to settle in the early stages of a race, but that is impossible with some horses.

One thing is for sure: Thoroughbreds straight out of racing will not be suitable for the average rider. That is where the new 'Racehorse to Riding Horse' classes come in, held around Ireland now and culminating in 'the big one' at the Dublin Horse Show in August. It has been highly successful in drawing the crowds and raising the profile of the sport. Instead of ex-racehorses being turned out in wet and muddy fields for the remainder of their days, or despatched into a dogfood can, skilled horsemen are putting hours of flat work into them, reschooling them and teaching them to go in a totally different way at a comparatively advanced age.

Some make good hacks or are re-educated for show-jumping, but one of the most popular roles for the ex-racehorse is to go hunting, and this can give years of highly satisfying retirement. This has been done for many racehorses all along. Also, increasingly, racehorse trainers teach their horses as youngsters to jump over poles and solid obstacles, to judge a stride and to balance themselves, and this also stands them in good stead after their time racing.

The first of the new Racehorse to Riding Horse classes was held in Dublin in 2009. Moscow Flyer had been retired for two years and behaved himself well under Barbara Morgan to finish fifth behind the newly retired Brave Inca. (Kicking King was fourth.) Unplaced only eight times out of thirty-five runs, which included a Champion Hurdle among his fifteen wins, Brave Inca was a credit to his Wexford trainer Colm Murphy. Incredibly brave and consistent, he was part of the heyday of Irish racing during the Celtic Tiger years when all big UK race prizes came across to Ireland at one time or another. Memorably, in 2005, all of the big four did: the Champion Hurdle (won by Hardy Eustace; Harchibald was a neck second, and Brave Inca another neck third), the Queen Mother Champion Chase (won by Moscow Flyer), the Cheltenham Gold Cup (won by Kicking King) and the Aintree Grand National (won by Hedgehunter). Brave Inca franked his lovely temperament by again winning the RDS class in 2011, this time with Mansony, Accordion Etoile and

Harchibald behind him. In 2010 it had been the turn of 2006 Gold Cup winner War of Attrition.

13

Hardy Eustace

W
hen Hardy Eustace won his first Champion Hurdle in 2004 at a price of 33–1, it was probably a surprise to most people bar those closest to him. When he won it again the following year, he proved that the initial victory had been no fluke. Hardy Eustace was one of those model horses, born to please – which is what he did throughout his racing career.

In the mid-1990s, Patrick Joyce was a fairly typical dairy farmer who also kept a National Hunt mare. On one of his regular visits to Cashel cattle market, a few miles from his home in Bal-lynonty, near Thurles, Co. Tipperary, he got chatting with Vere Hunt, who was looking to offload one of two barren mares for little money. It suited Patrick and Louise Joyce to have a companion for their mare, and a deal of £400 was agreed for the one called Sterna Star. Sterna Star had raced fourteen times on the flat for Curragh trainer Liam Browne, producing one win, by a head, in the Rose of Tralee Ladies race of 1988.

Patrick Joyce liked the mare and sent her to the sprinter Archway, at Coolmore Stud, in a foal-share arrangement with Bob Lanigan, who worked there, but she returned barren again. 'But I liked Archway. He had so much muscle on him,' Joyce recalls. He tried again, and the mare got in foal. The bay who was to be called Hardy Eustace was born on 5 April 1997.

Joyce was going to produce him for the flat, but nobody wanted to know about Archway, and so he called in vet John Halley to castrate him. The young bay was sedated, and Halley asked to see the colt walk. Wobbly from sedation, he still impressed the vet enough to ask the breeder why he wanted him gelded. 'I'm going to regret this,' Halley told his client. And he did.

When the now-gelding was a three-year-old, he was offered to a leading National Hunt trainer who rejected him, saying he 'wouldn't touch an Archway'. (Archway, incidentally, went to Australia, where he sired a number of Stakes and Group winners on the flat.) Such is the fickle nature and the fascination of commercial Thoroughbred breeding.

Trainer Dessie Hughes was driving to Thurles in November 2000 when he received a phone call from Louise Cooper-Joyce to say she had a couple of nice three-year-olds and would he like to drop by. Hughes, calm, seemingly unflappable, and himself a Champion Hurdle-winning jockey (on Monksfield in 1980), was immediately struck by the fine Archway bay with black points and no white on him. Even then it was clear he had an equable temperament.

'I liked his conformation but I knew little about the sire,' Hughes recalls. 'Then I looked up the dam's pedigree, and I loved it. It was very strong. The second dam had bred Star Appeal who won the Arc and the fourth dam had bred Strong Gale [who became one of the top National Hunt sires]. He was Germanbred, and very tough.'

The upshot was that, although Hughes declined the asking price of £30,000, he asked to be kept in touch should anyone else express an interest before the Goffs Land Rover Sale the following spring. Any horse purchased at this sale would be eligible to run in the prestigious Goffs Land Rover Bumper at Fairyhouse the following April. (This is now held at the Punchestown Festival.)

When the sale day arrived there were many other beautifully bred and good-looking prospective top-class National Hunt horses, among them one who was to be called Central House, who went home with Dessie Hughes that night for owner John Kenny, along with another, to be named Snug Decision. Central House would go on to win eight chases and to place in a further eighteen, all in the top echelons. He twice contested the Queen Mother Champion Chase. Snug Decision never won, gaining third in a hurdle and in a point-to-point.

Hughes had lined up owner Lar Byrne for the Archway gelding from the Joyces. Byrne was on holiday but gave him the nod to go up to £30,000. Byrne was not new to racing, and he knew all too well about the ups and downs of the sport. A Carlow businessman, he owned a few horses over the years. More recently he had a very good horse in Schindler's Hunt, who unfortunately was killed.

On the day of the sale, once more, no one seemed to like the sire, and Hughes had the future dual Champion Hurdler for £21,000. It wasn't just the bargain price that impressed him. The moment the bay came home to Osborne Lodge, surrounded by sheep on the Curragh, Hardy Eustace (named after a character from Tullow, Co. Carlow) was a model personality.

'He was very, very easy to break, and he rode off very quickly. He was a lovely character, and no matter what was going on he would just eat and sleep and do whatever he was asked to do – and loved doing it. He had loads of guts and was very healthy. It was only in his last couple of seasons that he had a bit of mucus trouble. I have never seen him throw a buck, he was always quiet, and he was very, very well made, a model, in good proportion, and, if anything, he got even better looking as he got older. He was 16.3 hands but never looked it because he was so well made.'

Hardy Eustace did get very strong, as Johnny Francome found when riding him on the gallops prior to his second Champion Hurdle, for Channel 4 Racing. As a baby no such strength or ability appeared in prospect.

Before long, Hardy Eustace and Central House were working together on the gallops, but it was Central House who showed more speed at home. Perhaps Hardy Eustace was just so laid back in attitude that he could appear lazy, but even that would be too strong a word for a horse for whom Hughes has no criticism. After a career spanning eight years, in which he would have crossed approximately 350 flights of hurdles, Hughes reckons Hardy Eustace was one of the quickest jumpers of a hurdle he has ever seen – 'Maybe even better than Monksfield.' He can recall just one – yes, only one – jumping error the horse ever made, and that was when a hurdle flicked back into him, having been knocked by the horse ahead. It was in Navan, and the leader was the amazing mare Solerina, belonging to the Bowes. She turned out for them hot on the heels of their phenomenal Limestone Lad, who won twenty-nine of his forty-seven hurdle races and placed in another fourteen from 1997 to 2003. He also won four of his six chases, yet jumped hesitantly and was reverted to hurdles. Then Solerina won eighteen of her twenty-nine hurdle races, from 2002 to 2006. What made the pair all the more remarkable was that they both nearly always won from out in front, almost invariably making all the running in their races.

While Central House was to go on to be a chaser in the top drawer, he began, like most National Hunt horses, with bumpers and hurdles. At this stage of his career he was considered the better of the Goffs Sales horses. In early March 2002, he contested a maiden hurdle and finished a promising third of ten in the hands of Kieran Kelly. He was on course for his next outing, the 'Land Rover' on 2 April.

A couple of weeks later, on 16 March, Hardy Eustace made his racecourse debut in a bumper at Punchestown, ridden by Roger Loughran. 'Hardy was learning as he went along and finished fifth of twenty-five so I decided he also deserved a tilt at the Land Rover race, although I still believed Central House was the better horse,' Hughes recalls.

Stable amateur Kevin O'Ryan was given the ride, while Roger Loughran was booked for Central House. Hughes also ran Snug

Decision in the twenty-five-runner line-up. As the race unfolded, Hughes became more and more confident that Central House was going to win. He improved from fourth to second and appeared to have the race for the taking, while Hardy Eustace was back in about tenth as they entered the finishing straight.

There was a big shock in store. One horse emerged from the pack in hot pursuit, staying on as the others were floundering. To the astonishment of Dessie Hughes, Hardy Eustace fairly sprinted down the straight to nab Central House and beat him by two lengths, with the favourite, Scarthy Lad, one and a half lengths back in third.

After this performance, it would have been fair to think of Hardy Eustace as a future staying star, and thoughts of the shorter, more prestigious Champion Hurdle would not enter his connections' heads for some while yet. That prestigious Fairyhouse success saw Hardy Eustace so well that he was given a crack at Punchestown's Champion bumper, in which he finished sixth, before heading off for his summer holidays with P. J. and Catherine Murphy, Lar Byrne's sister, in Westmeath.

The following July, returning home from the Galway Festival, Dessie Hughes's lorry dropped by to pick him up, a tradition that has continued to this day, including in retirement. He still spends his winters stabled and is ridden out daily rather than being left in a field in the worst of the weather.

Hardy Eustace's career settled into an easy routine: home from Westmeath in late July, quiet work at Osborne Lodge building up to an autumn racecourse reappearance, often in a 'warm-up' flat race first. The promise Hardy Eustace had shown by winning the Land Rover bumper was franked in his second season, 2003–4. After a good fifth of twenty-three in a 2-mile flat race at Navan for Niall McCullagh he began his hurdling career. Ridden by Kieran Kelly, he won a maiden hurdle (later disqualified on a technicality) and two novice hurdles (beating future chasers Back In Front and Nil Desperandum) before going under by two lengths to Solerina.

The next step was a crack at the 2 mile 5 furlongs Royal and Sun Alliance Novices Hurdle at the Cheltenham Festival. It was a big ask. Nineteen went to post, and when Hardy Eustace lost his place four flights from home he looked beaten. That was without reckoning on Hardy's staying power and also, in particular, his resolution. Young Kieran Kelly got down to work on him, and the horse responded so well that he was back in contention three out and actually took up the running at the penultimate flight. From there, his stamina and guts came into play, he galloped to a length victory over Pizarro, and he and his jockey returned to heroes' welcomes.

Kelly rode Hardy Eustace once more after his stunning Cheltenham win. Believing he was more a stayer than a Champion Hurdle type, he contested the 3 mile 1 furlong Martell Cognac Sefton Novices Chase at Aintree but finished a disappointing fifth. Four months later, on 8 August 2003, Kelly rode a winner at Kilbeggan, Barrack Buster, and went out in buoyant mood for the 3 mile 1 furlong Joe Coonan Memorial Handicap Chase for his guv'nor on eleven-year-old Balmy Native. He had ridden him eighteen times before, since July 1999, and had won on him twice, both times in chases at Downpatrick, in October 2001 and October 2002.

The form book says simply of the Kilbeggan race, 'second when fell five out'. It was one of those horrendous falls in which the young jockey was kicked in the head and then rolled on by the fallen horse. He never regained consciousness, and four days later, aged just twenty-five, he died. The horse never ran again. It had been the sixty-third run in his career, and he had only fallen once before – in a beginners chase at Kilbeggan also ridden by Kieran Kelly.

Poignantly, Kelly's first winner, in June 1996, had been on a horse called Angel From Heaven. He was the first jockey to be killed in a race in Ireland for seventeen years. In another bitter blow to the close-knit racing world, flat race apprentice Sean Cleary died at Galway later that summer.

On his reappearance in autumn 2003, Hardy Eustace did more than warm up in the 2-mile flat race at Navan: he won it, ridden by Niall McCullagh. Jockey Conor O'Dwyer took over in the saddle for his hurdle races, but Hardy was beaten at 4–1 on in his first and was then seventh of seven in the Grade 1 December Festival Hurdle at Leopardstown.

It was not an auspicious start to their pairing, but new tactics were tried when he attempted the Red Mills Trial Hurdle over 2 miles at Gowran Park, setting out to make all the running and using his proven stamina to test his rivals. In spite of a valiant effort, he was caught on the line, going under to Georges Girl by a short head.

The easier option might have been to go for the stayers race, the World Hurdle, at the Festival, but call it gut instinct, connections decided to attempt the Champion Hurdle itself. Without having attained a hurdle win that season, Hardy Eustace was sent off a 33–1 shot for the Smurfit Champion Hurdle. Once again, Conor

O'Dwyer set out to make all the running on him. As they cleared the penultimate flight, Conor got down to work. Of the other thirteen runners, only the title-holder, the grey Rooster Booster, was able to challenge, and he joined Hardy Eustace at the last flight in a perfectly timed run. To the viewers in the stands and in front of their televisions, the writing looked on the wall: Rooster Booster was about to pounce for his second Champion title. Hardy Eustace and Conor O'Dwyer had other ideas. Rallying to his rider's cajoling, the horse not only held off the champion but actually drew clear up that famous hill to finish five lengths ahead at the line. Apart from the celebrations there were, naturally, many tributes paid to the late Kieran Kelly, whose ride Hardy Eustace had been.

When Rooster Booster travelled over to Punchestown to take on Hardy Eustace again in Ireland's equivalent of the Champion Hurdle, there were many who thought the tables would be turned, and Rooster Booster was sent off 13–8 favourite. Also in the nine-strong field were Scarthy Lad, Solerina and Georges Girl. The only five-year-old in the race was Harchibald. But the race really was between the Champion 1–2. This time O'Dwyer settled Hardy in third place and took over the lead entering the home straight. Once again, in spite of being challenged, he held on resolutely to beat the grey by a length.

It was off to his well-deserved summer break for Hardy Eustace. He returned to the challenge of retaining his hurdling crown. He skipped his usual flat race and did not appear until Navan in December (the race won by Solerina in which Dessie Hughes remembers his one and only jumping error). He finished second, and in his next two runs at the big Leopardstown Christmas and

January meetings he was third to Jessica Harrington's Macs Joy. A dead easy 6–1-on victory at Gowran put Hardy in great heart for his bid to retain the Champion title, for which he started 7–2 joint favourite along with Back In Front.

This time there were some interesting new kids on the block, and the biggest talking point of all was the enigmatic Harchibald. Brave Inca was also in the field (10–1). Macs Joy, who had twice beaten Hardy was, like Harchibald, a 7–1 shot, and Essex, ridden by A. P. McCoy, was not unfancied at 9–1, while former champion Rooster Booster, now a veteran at eleven years of age, was out at 16–1 in the betting.

Conor O'Dwyer set out to dictate affairs on his willing partner. He knew he had speedy and potentially top-class rivals, and his aim, as ever, was to beat them on stamina. He also used considerable cunning – jockey craft – and didn't set a suicidal pace, for although he went out in front he kept enough up his sleeve. As Harchibald and Brave Inca (both to become two of Ireland's greatest hurdlers) challenged, he pulled out all the stops. Paul Carberry sat motionless on Harchibald, knowing he was not the sort of horse to respond to pressure. All he had to do was unleash an inch on the reins, and Harchibald would sweep by. Paul let out the notch; Harchibald did not respond. Brave Inca, setting the tone for future races and living up to his name, couldn't quite get there either. In as thrilling a Champion Hurdle finish as it is possible to imagine, the gallant Hardy Eustace won by a neck and a neck, and for the second time was crowned champion.

It was again December before he reappeared, this time for a facile victory at 8–1 on over Arthur Moore's gallant Native

Upmanship at Punchestown on New Year's Eve. A month later, he finished seventh of seven behind Brave Inca in the AIG Champion Hurdle at Leopardstown. The new kid on the block was staking his claim. Hurdling, generally, is a young horse's game, especially at the top end.

Six weeks later, attempting his third Smurfit Champion Hurdle, Hardy Eustace showed himself as gutsy as ever and truly went down fighting. He was fitted with a visor (similar to blinkers) for the first time, just to help him concentrate on the job in hand, to try and help him get home ahead of his rivals. He chased the leaders to halfway, where he gained the lead, but when Brave Inca joined him two out he made his rival fight every inch of the way. It was only on the run-in that he lost second and finished a far-from-disgraced fourth.

His season ended with a well-beaten second to the mare Asian Maze, who got Tom Mullins off to a great start in his training career, and then a third to Macs Joy at Punchestown for the ACC Bank Champion Hurdle at Ireland's National Hunt Festival.

He had an October appearance on the flat for the 2006–7 season. Dessie Hughes's son Richard took the Curragh ride. Attached to Richard Hannon's Wiltshire stable, both as stable jockey and son-in-law, Richard is one of the UK's most accomplished flat race jockeys. They started favourite but finished sixth of sixteen.

It was different next time. Now aged nine, Hardy travelled to Ascot for the 2½-mile Ascot Coral Hurdle, and he won so easily, beating his six rivals on a tight rein, that the camp knew their boy had not lost his ability. He was beaten next time by Detroit City, but that he had retained his relish for a fight was shown even more decisively at Leopardstown for the AIG Champion Hurdle. He showed all his old tenacity to see off Brave Inca in a drawn-out duel. Brave Inca joined and even passed him, but Hardy Eustace not only regained the lead, he went on to a three-length victory.

And so to the 2007 Champion Hurdle. Detroit City was sent off favourite, but it was 16–1 Irish shot Sublimity who took the honours, with Hardy an honourable fourth. His season ended with a third in the ACC Irish Champion Hurdle at Leopardstown.

For his flat race opener the following autumn the Irish Cesarewitch was chosen, finishing mid-division, then it was off to Ascot to win his second Coral Hurdle. He finished valiant seconds in his next three races, taking a similar route as usual to Cheltenham, but this time, now eleven, he was tilted at the World Stayers Hurdle, finishing mid-division.

Conor O'Dwyer retired, and for the 2008–9 season Paddy Flood took over in the saddle – to good effect. Hardy Eustace bypassed his initial flat race and went straight for the Grade 1 Maplewood Developments Hurdle at Punchestown in November. He was the outsider of the four runners at 14–1, but nobody told Hardy Eustace: he made the most of the running and, when headed, fought back determinedly. No one could have guessed it would be his last win, but advancing years were inevitably blunting his speed against younger rivals.

Rather than try the World Hurdle again, connections sent him to where he loved the best: the Smurfit Champion Hurdle. Hardy Eustace tried as hard as ever, but he had no answer for the likes of Punjabi, as reflected in his starting price of 100–1.

On New Year's Eve 2009, the day before his official twelfth

birthday, Hardy Eustace ran second to Footy Facts in a comparatively modest hurdle at Punchestown. The ground was heavy, and he tried his heart out, as always, but it was a race that in his younger days he would have won by a country mile. Trainer Dessie Hughes called time on the horse that had given him two Champion Hurdles among his fourteen wins in addition to seventeen placings. 'We were very lucky,' Dessie says, 'we were doing OK but he put us up on a higher plane, and a lot of new owners came to us on the back of him.' No one could have deserved that more than Dessie Hughes, who has seen both sides of the racing coin.

For Hardy Eustace, retirement has meant routine without the racing: summers at grass in Westmeath and winters in Dessie Hughes's stables, where he is ridden daily, but not asked for strenuous work. Throughout his honourable career he remained the model horse.

14

Makybe Diva

The alarm clock penetrated the sleepy haze at 3.45 a.m., Tuesday, 1 November 2005. The first Tuesday in November. For Southern Hemisphere racing folks, and a good few in the Northern Hemisphere, that means one thing: the Melbourne Cup.

Woke up. Turned on the TV. Was hoping to see an Irish winner in Jim Sheridan's valiant Vinnie Roe, trained by Dermot Weld, who had two Melbourne Cups to his credit already (Vintage Crop and Media Puzzle). Instead, I witnessed one of my greatest racing moments: a magnificent three-timer by a legendary Australian mare called Makybe Diva.

It was hot in Australia that November, as might be expected, and, with the ground dry, the Makybe Diva team had let it be known that she would not run if the Flemington track, in the Melbourne suburbs, remained unwatered. It was watered.

Nothing could stop the heat, and, after the race, a number of horses were dehydrated.

Vinnie Roe and Makybe Diva were joint top weights of the twenty-four runners on 9 stone 2 pounds. It was also Vinnie Roe's third attempt at the A$1.25 million Emirates-sponsored contest, his first having been in 2002 when he lost second place in the dying strides to finish fourth behind his stable mate Media Puzzle. He was not there in 2003 when Makybe Diva scored her first win, and in 2004 he finished a gallant second to her. That year, the four-time Irish St Leger winner Vinnie Roe started at 50–1, and the mare was 17–5 favourite.

In Australia, Melbourne Cup Day stops the nation. Shops, offices, factories and schools are closed, and those people who can't be part of the 100,000-plus crowd at Flemington Racecourse will find their way to a television, 10 million viewers in all, probably while they are also enjoying a 'barbie' in the sun with their friends.

At last the throngs of crowds resplendent in their finery stopped milling around and let out a simultaneous cheer as the stalls opened. The 2005 running of Australia's great race was under way, led first by Portland Singa and then by Mr Celebrity.

The mare's jockey Glen Boss knew halfway through the 2-mile race that he had a lot of horse under him, and, in spite of the weight, he was already confident of winning. For Vinnie Roe, by contrast, the writing was on the wall even before the start as he had the worst draw of all, number 24. Those close to Vinnie Roe felt he ran as good a race as any in his honourable career, finishing a fast-closing eighth.

It was all about Makybe Diva. She had lobbed along on the inside rail in the early stages but when pulled out, 3 furlongs from home, she made relentless progress and overtook Portland Singa with a furlong to go. On A Jeune and Xcellent, both even wider, tried to go with her.

Makybe Diva was not for beating. The crowd of 106,479 began cheering, their voices rising to a crescendo. In a few devastating strides the race was over and the mare had galloped into the history books. A jockey will only seldom hear the crowds during a race, but Glen Boss heard them that time.

In the little town of Mansfield, two hours north-east of Melbourne, Patsy and Peter Smiles attended a local bush-race meeting. Peter, now retired, is a former Director of Security for the Jockey Club in Great Britain. Mansfield is tucked below the Victorian Alps section of the Great Dividing Range and better known for cattlemen (including the infamous Ned Kelly) and skiing on nearby Mount Buller than horse racing. The Mansfield District Racing Club hosts two meetings a year, the other being on St Stephen's Day.

My sister, Patsy, remembers that historic race: 'We were at a tent at Mansfield bush racing on that famous day. We all crowded around the little TV in the tent, and the commentary was coming over the tannoy. As you can imagine there was a huge roar all around when she surged through just after they'd hit the straight.

When she won, carrying all that weight too, we were all hugging everyone around, and lots of friends who were just there for the social fun and didn't know anything about racing were also carried away by the excitement!'

It was during the protracted and memorable post-race celebrations that Makybe Diva's owner, Tony Šantić, holding aloft the treasured trophy, announced the heroine's retirement. She had come a long, long way from her modest fourth placing on her racing debut, in a 6-furlong £1,000 race at a country meeting at Benalla three years before. For all that, she won her next six races in a row, the last one worth £42,000, the Grade 2 Queen Elizabeth Stakes over 13 furlongs at Flemington.

It was not such plain sailing in 2003. She failed to win a race before the Melbourne Cup, but her price of 7–1 suggested she was not unfancied among the twenty-three runners, and she beat She's Archie comfortably enough. Her trainer, David Hall, left to work in Hong Kong, and she was trained for the remainder of her career by Lee Freedman, who had already produced three previous Melbourne Cup winners. Before the 2004 Melbourne Cup there had been only one win and two seconds, of a head and a short head, but she started favourite, and she showed a swifter turn of foot to beat Vinnie Roe in driving rain.

Before the 2005 race she was as impressive as ever (bar two abortive runs in Japan), winning three of her four races, including the Cox Plate, and going under by a short head in the other. No wonder the atmosphere at Flemington was electric before, during and after the 2005 Melbourne Cup. There were incredible scenes after her win as the Aussies went wild, saluting, waving and cheering. Makybe Diva was their heroine, the first horse, let alone the first mare, ever to win the Melbourne Cup three times. To put that into some sort of perspective, it probably equates to Red Rum's third Grand National – and then some more. (The last mare to win the Grand National was Nickel Coin in 1951.) Even Red Rum's historic feat did not produce the scenes that followed Makybe Diva's incredible achievement.

Makybe Diva is one of only five horses to have won the Cup more than once in the long history of the event, which was first run in 1861. The others were Archer, who won the first two runnings in 1861 and 1862, Peter Pan (1932 and 1934), Rain Lover (1968 and 1969) and Think Big (1974 and 1975). She is also the only mare among the list of multiple winners and one of only fourteen mares or fillies to have won the Cup.

Better known and remembered than these dual winners, worthy as they were, are Phar Lap and Carbine, two Australian legends, along with Crisp in more recent times for his heroic defeat on Red Rum's first Grand National; Crisp never ran in the Melbourne Cup but won a number of Australian steeplechases before travelling to England.

Phar Lap, bred in New Zealand, was exceptionally big for a flat racehorse. He won the 1930 Melbourne Cup, after being shot at on the gallops earlier in the week. He won thirty-seven of his fifty-one races, showing a blistering speed, but was found dead in his stable from poisoning when he was racing in California. After his death he was found to have a heart weighing twice that of average.

When Carbine won the thirty-nine-runner 1890 Melbourne Cup he was carrying 10 stone 5 pounds. The runner-up received

53 pounds (just 3 pounds less than 4 stone). In what makes it an even more worthy feat, Carbine scored in record time. He won thirty-three of his forty-three starts and was unplaced just once. Also New Zealand bred, he spent his early stud years Down Under but when, five years after his memorable Cup win, he was bought by the Duke of Portland and exported to England, some 2,000 fans lined the docks to bid him farewell. And, what's more, he sired the 1906 Derby winner Spearmint.

But back to the 2005 Melbourne Cup.

I remained glued to the television long after the race as the jubilations continued, forgetting the main reason for the early viewing (Vinnie Roe). There was so much to this victory. Not only was it the first time any horse had won the historic race three times, but also this was a mare who had failed to sell as a youngster.

Her story begins in Ireland, where her dam, American-bred Tugela, by Riverman out of a mare by Roberto, visited Irish Derby and Irish 2000 Guineas winner Desert King at Coolmore Stud, Co. Tipperary. Ironically, given that he went on to sire one of the greatest stayers in Makybe Diva, Desert King was perceived to have stamina limitations and was not aimed at the Irish St Leger, which would have given him the Irish Triple Crown.

Although well bred, Tugela's own racing career was inauspicious, to say the least. Trained by Barry Hills in Lambourn, she ran just twice as a two-year-old in maidens, finishing fifth of nine at Beverley over 7 furlongs, and twelfth of eighteen over a mile at Doncaster. She was nicely bred, and once in foal she was sent to the December 1998 Tattersalls Sales in Newmarket where she was bought by bloodstock agent John Foote on behalf of one Tony

Šantić, an entrepreneurial tuna fisherman, for 60,000 guineas. Like others of Šantić's British-bought horses, the new purchase was sent to Dick Fowlston's Britton House Stud, near Crewkerne in Somerset, for foaling, and on 21 March 1999, at just after midnight, a bay filly was born.

After weaning the following autumn, the foal was sent to the Tattersalls Foal Sales, but she failed to reach her reserve and was not sold. She returned to Somerset where she grazed with other youngsters until the following summer, when she and her mother were shipped to Australia. There, the six-month difference in seasons would render the filly, now a yearling, unable to run in top age-related events such as the Australian Oaks.

There are five women in Australia whose names are inextricably entwined with the mare: Maureen, Kylie, Belinda, Diane and Vanessa all worked for Šantić. With Tugela's foal unsold and now on Australian soil, he had to name her. This is often done by using aspects of the sire's and dam's names, but Šantić did it by taking the first two letters from each of those women's names.

Tony Šantić is one of those colourful characters who add so much to the worldwide racing tableau. His racing silks are colourful, too, and many of the mare's fans sported their red, white and blue at her last Cup. By the time of her historic third Cup win, Šantić acknowledged that she had '20 million owners', and since her retirement he has continued to keep in touch with her fans via her own website.

Makybe Diva possessed that greatest of racing qualities: heart. She was unable to run in the classics because of the hemisphere difference so that meant that as she climbed up the handicap she had to give away more and more weight to her rivals. Yet she still won fifteen of her thirty-six races and placed in another seven.

She fully deserved all the accolades heaped upon her. At the end of the 2005–6 season she was named Australian Champion Racehorse of the Year for the second time, becoming just the third horse to win that accolade more than once. She was also named Australian Champion Stayer, winning this award for the third consecutive year as well as Australian Champion Middle Distance Racehorse. In 2006, the inaugural Spirit of Sport Award (for 2005) was given to Makybe Diva and her connections (Lee Freedman, Tony Šantić and Glen Boss) by the Sport Australia Hall of Fame for her three successive Melbourne Cups. She was also inducted into the Australian Racing Hall of Fame, and it was announced that she would be honoured at Flemington Racecourse with a bronze statue. A life-sized bronze statue was also erected on the foreshore in Šantić's home town of Port Lincoln, South Australia. In 2007, the Craiglee Stakes (a Group 2 over 1,600 metres at Flemington in September) was renamed the Makybe Diva Stakes. She was truly a 'one off'. She went off to stud and a life in the breeding paddocks, having won an Australian record of $14,526,685 in prize money.

Her three-quarter brother, by Redoute's Choice, had been sold in April 2005 for an Australian record price of $2.5 million. Subsequently named Musket, the colt won his debut at Canterbury in August 2006, and in 2008 won the Grade 2 Shannon Stakes at Rosehill.

What sort of figures would the Diva's progeny make in the sales rings or achieve on the track? There was not too long to wait to find out. Her first mating was with Epsom Derby winner Galileo at Coolmore Stud's Hunter Valley branch in New South Wales. At 3.16 a.m. on the morning of 17 August 2007, she gave birth to her first foal, to be called Rockstardom. He was subsequently sold for $1.5 million while her second foal, a filly by Fusaichi Pegasus, to be named La Dolce Diva, was knocked down for $1.2 million. Šantić has retained the third, a colt by Encosta De Lago, on his Makybe Stud near Geelong in Victoria.

Rockstardom finished fourth on his debut in August 2010 – just as his mother had done. He finally got off the mark on his eighth attempt in November 2011. La Dolce Diva was down the field in her first four starts. In August 2011, the great mare Makybe Diva produced her fourth foal, a colt by Australian champion sire, Lonhro.

15

Zenyatta

While watching Makybe Diva's historic third Melbourne Cup ranks as one of my great racing moments, Zenyatta's final run rates as one of the worst (barring fatal falls, which are worst of all). Zenyatta should have ended her sensational career unbeaten. That she failed was not, I contend, her fault. The hype surrounding her last appearance was, in modern parlance, 'unreal'. Surrounded by crowds and cameras as if she had already won, from early in the morning on the gallops, in the stable and up until she was let out onto the course, the mare acted even more like a prima donna than usual. (The name 'Diva' would have been more appropriate for her!) Even as she was being led out, jockey Mike Smith on her back, she was not so much prancing as throwing herself to the ground, striking out with her front legs and giving a close resemblance of numerous curtsies. None of this would have stopped her winning. The temperament that Zenyatta displayed was more of the show-off type than capricious – 'Look at me and bow, for I'm the Queen.'

Crowds can have a huge effect on some horses, and I remain convinced that Dawn Run was so affected by the euphoric cheers, waving, singing and barging of the crowds after her incredible Cheltenham Gold Cup win that the very next time out, in what is now the Martell Cup Chase at Aintree, she was so hyped up – doubtless anticipating more of the same adulation – that she simply 'missed out' the first fence altogether. She was lucky not to have been killed. When, a couple of months later, she broke her neck in France, she had been jumping impeccably. She had gone into every previous obstacle level with a rival but had jumped so well that each time she landed two lengths up, until that fatal mishap.

Zenyatta, of course, had no jumps to contend with. Always ridden from the rear, the giant mare – she stood 17.2 hands, massive for a flat horse – was at one time in her last race virtually tailed off behind her rivals. It was the six-year-old brown mare's twentieth race, and she had won all nineteen previous contests. Nor had they been mere minor events. From her third run on they had all been Grades 1 or 2. Mike Smith, riding for trainer John Shirreffs and owners Mr and Mrs Jerome S. Moss, took over for Zenyatta's last seventeen rides, and time and time again the pair ran the early stages of each race from the rear. She would then be steered around her rivals, from where she would greedily eat up the clear ground ahead of her and gallop to victory, sometimes in heart-stopping fashion but always getting there in time.

In 2008, as a four-year-old, she won the Breeders' Cup Ladies Classic at Santa Anita, and the following year, with the Breeders' Cup Festival again held in the Californian sunshine, she stepped up to the Breeders' Cup Classic, worth more than $2 million. With the benefit of hindsight, it was very similar to her final run, but with a better outcome: she missed the break, was sixth (of twelve) entering the straight, was pulled out wide and took the lead about 70 yards before the line to beat the useful Gio Ponti by a length.

A year later, the Breeders' Cup was back in Churchill Downs. The meeting rotates around various American tracks. It was founded in 1984 by John R. Gaines of Lexington, Kentucky, whose avowed intention was to make it a 'global Thoroughbred Olympics', and, in spite of the uniform flat left-handed oval of American tracks and the fact that horses there are allowed to run on drugs, the concept has been an undoubted success – with the best of Europe and the rest of the world taking on the Americans at their own game and often bringing home the prizes, which are worth millions of dollars.

Each race is a championship finale in its own right, from sprints, to races for mares and fillies, with contests on Turf as well as on dirt, and all culminating in the Breeders' Cup Classic on dirt run over 10 furlongs. By 1988, four years after its inauguration, Breeders' Cup Day was worth $10 million, the single richest day in racing in the world. Today, the various purses range from $500,000 to $5 million per race. The Dubai World Cup carries a purse of $10 million, while the Japan Cup is approximately $5 million.

The 2010 Breeders' Cup Classic drew twelve starters, with Zenyatta at a shade odds-on. The race began much as usual, so much so that when the commentator announced Zenyatta had come out of the gates 'dead last' the crowds gave a laugh that was almost a jeer, for last, after all, was what Zenyatta did. Then things became even more dramatic than usual. She wasn't just last but was a full twenty lengths behind the last of the eleven horses in front of her. When she did respond to Mike Smith, she came up behind a wall of horses, the dirt they kicked up hitting her in the face. She didn't like it. Pulled wide, she at last got into her giant stride, devouring the ground and picking off her rivals like over-ripe grapes. She stormed up the home stretch and looked on the point of overtaking the leader. The winning post came just too soon, and Zenyatta was beaten a head. Perhaps the biggest irony of all was that the winner's name was Blame.

Zenyatta was by Street Cry out of the American mare Vertigineux, by Kris (who was by Roberto), and like many of her family on both sides of her pedigree, she was a deep brown colour. So why does the name Street Cry ring a bell?

The look of utter disconsolation, dismay, disappointment – sheer 'guttedness' – was all too apparent on former champion jockey Ryan Moore's face when he rode in after the 2011 Epsom Derby. He had been riding the favourite; more than that, the owner had been trying ever since 1953 to win the great race since her Aureole in that year had been beaten by Pinza; and more than anything, he wanted to ride the winner for Her Majesty the Queen.

Irish interest had been ignited by the recent highly successful visit of the octogenarian monarch to Ireland. Carlton House was her ninth Derby runner and her best chance since Aureole; the date, 2 June 2011, coincided with the fifty-fourth anniversary of her coronation. Nothing went right for Carlton House; there was an injury scare in the lead-up to the race, and in running he was slightly hampered and was switched towards the outside five furlongs out. Eighth entering the straight, he was doing his best to catch the leaders when he lost a shoe. But, truth to tell, in Pour Moi he came up against a better horse.

And why mention Carlton House along with Zenyatta? Because they share the same sire, the Irish-bred Street Cry. Bred by Sheik Mohammed's Darley operation, owned by Godolphin and trained by Saeed Bin Suroor, Street Cry was by Machiavellian out of a mare by Troy; he was never unplaced in his races from two to four years, winning five and placing in seven, all of them in America, over 6 to 10 furlongs.

Zenyatta was trained in Hollywood Park, California, by Vietnam veteran and lifelong racing enthusiast John Shirreffs. Her regular farrier there was Irish-born Tom Halpenny, who hails from Ardee, Co. Louth. In 'her' internet diary (www.zenyatta. com), Zenyatta writes, 'Tom Halpenny was my blacksmith while racing. He is a lovely Irish gentleman who has worked in this field and been around many very accomplished race horses his entire life. Tom would work with John on my feet . . . and they would constantly be reviewing how my shoes would be customized just for my needs. This is a real skill and a blacksmith is extremely important to a horse!'

After her final run, the only race she ever lost, Zenyatta was retired to stud. She miscarried to 2006 Preakness champion

Bernardini, but a year later, 2012, she produced a colt, as she records in her 'diary'.

> I think this fortunate foal is blessed to have the most GODPARENTS of anyone in history. I truly can't THANK YOU enough for the way you have embraced both of US . . . ME for so many years . . . and now my 'Dumpling'.
>
> Many of you have asked about HIS NAME. At this time, my colt does not have an official name. Per the standard practice in our industry, he is referred to as '12 Zenyatta'. His halter tag reads this way indicating year born . . . and Mom's name. I know Ann and Jerry so well and can only imagine how many countless hours they will spend discussing this to make sure he has the perfect name. I trust their judgment completely!
>
> The most fun he and I've shared so far is when he 'takes off' to run in the paddock. Just like in MY RACING CAREER, I give him a head start (on purpose) . . . and then I catch him in a FLASH! This is one FUN GAME we play . . . and I'm loving every single stride.[1]

As I write, she is in foal again, this time to Tapit, a grey stallion who was trained in America by Michael Dickinson and now stands at stud in Lexington, Kentucky, for a fee of currently $125,000. He includes American champions and Breeders' Cup winners among his progeny.

---

1   Zenyatta's Diary, 13 March 2012, Diary Post No. 457, http://www.zenyatta.com/diary/diary-post-457 (accessed 31 May 2012).

So, while it is left to Zenyatta's offspring to try and carry on their dam's incredible race record, the mantle for the distaff side in the racing world has been handed over to the so-far-unbeaten mare, Black Caviar. Like Makybe Diva, she hails from Australia, but whereas the triple Melbourne Cup winner was a stayer, Black Caviar is a sprinter.

She is by Bel Esprit, a Royal Academy stallion who won two of his twelve sprints in Australia, both Group 1. Royal Academy, by Nijinsky, was trained by Vincent O'Brien to win four of his seven races. Memorably, in his last one, the Breeders' Cup Mile (Turf) he was ridden by Lester Piggott to get up by a neck, Lester having come back from retirement just twelve days previously. Black Caviar's unraced dam, Helsinge, was by the English horse, Desert Sun, who won two non-graded races and stood at the National Stud, Newmarket, for a fee of just £5,000. According to the Racing Post website, he 'can get useful 2-year-old winners, runners progress well.' His Sunline won seventeen races; otherwise his UK winners were in single figures.

Now six years old, Black Caviar has finally been given the world recognition that is her due, and on 12 May 2012, she scored her twenty-first consecutive victory, ridden by Luke Nolen in eighteen of those. It was her eleventh Group 1 win, along with seven at Group 2. Habitually starting at long odds-on, four of her recent starts have been at 1–20, one at 1–25 and one at 1–33; among these was an occasion when she 'only' started at 1–10 – and these are in the highest grade of races.

Never has there been more hype about a visiting international horse than there was for Black Caviar – Nelly – at Royal

Ascot 2012. She had travelled the thirty-hour 10,000-plus-mile trip wearing a special 'space' suit. Security on the one hand and press interest on the other were the most intense ever witnessed, and the Australian team had even brought over their own stalls handler to tend to her down at the start, sporting the salmon with black spots of her owners' colours. Not only did he lead her into the stalls but he then stayed with her on the stalls' bars, stroking her ears and literally whispering sweet nothings into them, until the moment of the off for the Group 1 Diamond Jubilee Stakes.

Some 7,000 Australians packed into Royal Ascot's gracious enclosures – about a tenth of the total. Many of them had come especially from Australia. Another 1,000 or so thronged Federation Square in Melbourne on a bitterly cold night, 12.45 a.m. their time, to watch the race unfold on the big screen.

Black Caviar, sporting her own winter coat, had been drawn on the wide outside, but she didn't let that detract from her chances because she was out of the stalls like a bolt and instantly into her long ground-devouring stride, at first handy, soon sharing the lead and not long later moving effortlessly to the front. Doing just enough.

Were the whips up on those behind, as Luke Nolen never touched his on the 'Wonder from Down Under'? Not entirely. There is a furlong to go. She doesn't scorch to the lead like Frankel did so sensationally on the opening day, but then this is a sprint, after all. There's 100 yards to go; it's in the can. Twenty yards out, and Luke Nolen drops his hands, stops riding, race done. He appears unaware that two horses are sprinting up the inside. Are we about to observe the 'Blunder from Down Under'? With precisely four strides left, the jockey suddenly realises he has to ride some more, and, in a momentous surge from the mare with truly no time left to do it in, she rallies courageously. No one knows if she has hung on; many believe that she – sorry, the jockey – has lost it. Have we just witnessed another Zenyatta?

Certainly, had the verdict gone the wrong way, Luke Nolen would have faced a lengthy suspension for 'dropping his hands' before the finish – and there are those who say he could never have returned to Australia! But at last the result of the photo finish came. Black Caviar had won her twenty-second race – deservedly – from twenty-two starts. As the jockey admitted afterwards of his 'brain fade': that you don't do that (drop your hands) – ever – is drummed into every apprentice jockey (and amateurs, for that matter).

And, rounding off a truly momentous Royal Ascot amid the Diamond Jubilee celebrations, HM Queen Elizabeth II (who fittingly had had a winner the previous day in the Queen's Vase), took the unprecedented step of coming down to the winner's enclosure to stroke the nose of someone else's horse. Black Caviar was literally 'presented' to her. As one wag put it: two queens together.

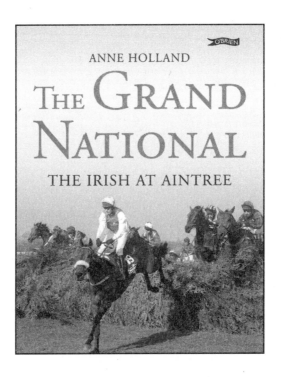

The Grand National
The Irish at Aintree
by Anne Holland

The Aintree Grand National is the world's most famous horserace –
fast-paced, exhilarating and occasionally perilous. Everyone – serious
racing fraternity and occasional flutterers alike – has heard of it.
Millions are staked on the race, and millions watch. Down through
the years it has produced many a fairytale result.

This lavishly-illustrated book examines the Irish presence at Aintree
from the festival's earliest years; Irish horses, jockeys, trainers and
breeders have always been prominent. No two horses have ever been
trained alike for Aintree and no two stories have ever been the same.
They are all here, written with the attention to detail and enthusiasm
of a true racing fanatic. A wide-ranging and compulsively readable
account of a beloved institution.

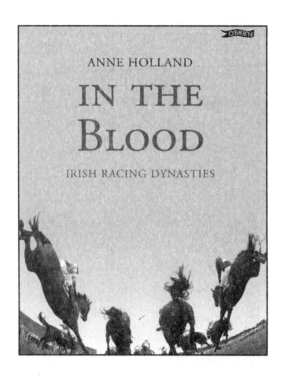

In the Blood
Irish Racing Dynasties
by Anne Holland

A golden thread links diverse equine and human characters in Irish racing, past and present: generations of families in which racing is truly in the blood – or one-off fanatics who acquire it in their veins.

Not only trainers and jockeys but also owners, breeders and the unsung heroes who care for their equine stars are portrayed here, as well as commentators and bookmakers, without whom the industry would be no more than a sideshow, instead of one of Ireland's greatest global products.

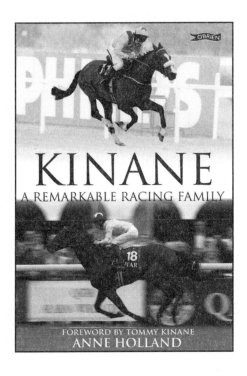

Kinane
A Remarkable Racing Family
by Anne Holland

Three generations of journeymen jump jockeys and one Flat world champion: no less than twenty of the Tipperary Kinane family have ridden in races; on and off the track they maintain a high work ethos – many have worked in Ballydoyle and still do, and Aidan O'Brien values them highly.

From humble beginnings with many mouths to feed, theirs is a story of hard work, gambles, injuries, unsung heroes, bad luck and good luck, and ones that got away. Tommy Kinane broke his neck in a fall, managed to ride in the next race by slapping his face to keep awake – and won it.